The Power of Horses
Youth Activity Book

Written by Kim Marie Wood

Illustrated by Kimberly Spatrisano Graham

Syncopated

PRESS

Where in the World?

Dozens of unique horse breeds are found throughout the world. Some breeds were the result of selective breeding by humans. Other breeds developed their individual characteristics in order to survive in their surroundings. Where did horses come from, anyway?

The origin of the horse we know today can be traced back almost 60 million years. Scientists have found fossil horse skeletal remains in many locations across the North American continent. The oldest equine ancestor was called ***Eohippus***, the **Dawn Horse**. Little ***Eohippus*** only weighed around twelve pounds and was as big as a medium sized dog. He had four toes on each front foot and three toes on each hind foot. (Hooves developed much later.) Archeologists know from fossil evidence that ***Eohippus*** was a leaf-browsing animal that lived in damp jungle-like conditions.

Eohippus

After ***Eohippus*** came ***Mesohippus*** and ***Miohippus***. Both of these equine ancestors lived between 25-40 million years ago. They both were a little bigger and had longer legs than ***Eohippus***. They had three toes on each foot, with more weight carried on the middle toe.

Something big happened in North America between 10 and 25 million years ago. The jungle-like conditions gradually changed and became open treeless plains. The horse's main food source changed from leafy jungle greenery to low growing grasses. To survive in this new situation, horses developed teeth suited for grazing and a longer neck to make it easier to graze. Horses were more open to attack by predators on the plains. Over millions of years, the position of a horse's eyes also adapted to give it a wider range of vision. Since a horse needed speed to flee from predato attacks, their legs also grew longer over time ar a single toe or hoof developed. The first single-hoofed horse was ***Pliohippus***, which lived in North America around six million years ago.

The true horse we know today, ***Equus caballus*** became established in North America around one million years ago. No one can say exactly why Equus disappeared from the North Americ continent about 10,000 years ago. Perhaps it ha something to do with the retreating glaciers fro the Ice Age. But before Equus disappeared fron North America, horses managed to migrate to Europe and Asia over land bridges that connect North America to Asia. Horses did not return to North America until Spanish explorers broug them in the 1500's.

The Mongolian Wild Horse, also known as Przewalski's Horse, is the only truly wild breed of horse that survives today. It has remained almost unchanged since the Ice Age. Because th breed was isolated for centuries, it maintains its protective camouflage coloring: dun with a dor stripe along its spine and zebra stripes on its le The Mongolian Wild Horse was hunted for me for centuries. Now nearly extinct, the Chinese and Russian governments are working to prese the breed. In an attempt to prevent extinction this equine treasure, the Mongolian Wild Hors can be seen in zoos around the world.

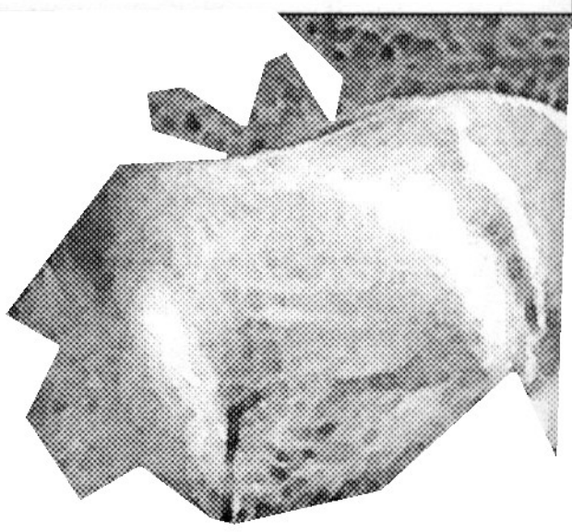

50 Breeds from Around the World

O N N F I J S H U Q P N A T I N K S C L L W P R U V X C P H
K B R C V L M V C R V P J R S D P F M H G N Z T J O T W P U
W G I T S O K Y N O P L L E F O X R H A F L I N G E R Q A Y
Q L A I E H H A R A B I A N N Y L I R C L Y D E S D A L E W
B H I H X N A H L X T W X I E I N Y G C N F P T R Q K C W E
L U S I T A N O D Q F M A E R A C O O O P U A U K E E A D E
S S P X P I O E D C S Y I T I J K I P Y G C P G E K H Y M W
I E T U U S V T S X B P C S H V I R B D W U V K G H N S D A
J L X G A U E I Q S D L E L S O O C R V N N A D L K E G H Q
S D M W N L R U G D E I T O N O R W E G I A N F J O R D B B
O S A P N A I S U V R E P H M P U O S L K F L M T R F S P M
L U R Q F D A P E F B P W T U T C R U L A T V H I W Y F F W
B R E T O N N L D L E E R A Y M A E I G U N A J G M D K U I
W N M B Y A A M R H L A U R L S S G Z F H E D B R I Q S R S
Z H M I A N L C B S D E E M V K P O F L O B U I L A H F I C
X Q A N D S O B H D D N F O A W I Z V G F X R G C K A Y O P
S O N B T F H P P O A M E R I C A N Q U A R T E R H O R S E
D K A K F P O K D Z S Q Q G A F N B G O Y Y G R D A O B O R
N Y N S O N B G I N N H D A L N K Q R H O Y F P O L M R F C
H L H F Y N O P A R A M E N N O C E X Q O V U Y R T K A S H
G N B G N T P S C C C L S T A N D A R D B R E D H E T B C E
S I T E Z I K L K V I U T G N N K S I E T Y S T E K M E Y R
B F C O L D E N B U R G R E A G R O B S K I R E D E R F R O
L J E Z E G E W O G E T P L H L N O B F G I S B R S M V G N
J T P K J Y I S C J M U R F Y S I A N N E D R A T S K S B I
H K K H W W R A F V A E G S I C N H T M H S L Y F Y J T E S
X Z M V V Z V Y N I D R A B A K V V S S I H W W O J Q L X N
Z V B T X F E A T L I X E B R I L N N J U A H R V L H R O V
X P Q B M K E Q E Q O L R Y J D D P U M Q M S Y Q C H Z O G
P V U Q F T J G Q K V E V M I B S D Q Y C Y X J G A T H U N

Akhal Teké
American Quarter Horse
American Saddlebred
Andalusian
Appaloosa
Arabian
Ardennais
Barb
Bashkir Curly
Belgian
Breton
Camargue
Caspian
Cleveland Bay
Clydesdale
Connemary Pony
Dartmoor Pony
Don
Fell Pony
Frederiksborg
Friesian
Furioso
Gelderlander
Hackney
Haflinger
Hanoverian
HighlandPony
Holsteiner
Icelandic Horse
Kabardin
Knabstrup
Lippizaner
Lusitano
Maremmana
Missouri Fox Trotter
Morgan
Mustang
Norwegian Fjord
Oldenburg
Percheron
Peruvian Paso
Selle Francais
Shetland Pony
Shire
Standardbred
Suffolk Punch
Tennessee Walking Horse
Thoroughbred
Trakehner
Welsh Pony

Made in America

By Kim Marie Wood and Elizabeth Wood

Did you know that there are more than 180 different breeds of horses in the world? American ingenuity has had a big influence on the equine world. There are many breeds of horses that were MADE IN AMERICA. These horses have also played an important part in the history of the United States.

The Mustang, a truly wild horse, can be found roaming free in many parts of the western United States today. The name Mustang came from the Spanish word "mestenya," meaning "lost sheep." Mustangs originated from domestic horses that escaped when the Spaniards brought them to North America in the 1600's. This horse helped settle the American West. At the beginning of this century there were an estimated 1 million Mustangs in the wild.

British settlers in Virginia began importing horses from England in the early 1600's. In addition to farm work, these settlers enjoyed racing their horses on a quarter-mile track, which is where the Quarter Horse breed got its name. English horses were crossed with the hardy Mustangs already in America to form the popular breed we know today. In the American West, the Quarter Horse became the perfect cow pony because of its speed, balance, agility and disposition.

The Appaloosa is one of the most colorful American breeds. The Nez Percé Indians developed the Appaloosa in the 18th century. Their foundation stock was also the wild Spanish Mustangs, which often carried the spotting gene. The Nez Percé lived in north-east Oregon, in the fertile valleys near the Palouse River, which is where the name Appaloosa came from. Early settlers called it "a Palouse" horse. In 1876, U.S. troops seized tribal lands and the Appaloosa was almost lost forever. Quarter horse blood was used to help preserve and revive the Appaloosa.

Another popular American breed is the Pony of the Americas (POA). The first POA was foaled in 1954, out of an Appaloosa mare and by a Shetland Pony stallion. The POA is pony-size, but with horse conformation and Appaloosa coloring.

The founding stallion of the Morgan horse was Justin Morgan, named after his school-master owner. Originally named Figure, this amazing horse was foaled in Massachusetts in 1789. He never lost a race or hauling contest, and was "pre-potent," meaning he was able to pass his desirable qualities on to his off-spring. The American Saddlebred, Tennessee Walking Horse, Quarter Horse and Standardbred all carry some Morgan blood.

The American Standardbred is a supreme harness racer. The name of the breed derives from the speed standard required to enter the breed registry. Another pre-potent stallion, Messenger, was the founding sire. Messenger was a Thoroughbred imported from England. The conformation of this breed allows great propulsion and speed. Many Standardbreds can cover a one-mile course in less than two minutes.

The American Saddlebred was originally called the Kentucky Saddler. It was devel-oped in the southern U.S. in the 1800's by crossing the Canadian Pacer and the

Narragansett Pacer. (These two minor breeds no longer exist today.) Later, Morgan and Thoroughbred blood was introduced. The Saddlebred has a showy but comfortable gait, which can carry a person in great comfort over long distances.

The Tennessee Walking Horse is a product of Thoroughbred, Standardbred, Morgan and American Saddlebred bloodlines. Developed by Tennessee farmers in the 19th century, the result was a horse that performed an unusual and smooth gait known as the "running walk."

The Missouri Foxtrotter is another gaited horse "MADE IN AMERICA." This breed was established in the Ozark Mountains of Missouri and Arkansas in the early 1800's. Early settlers interbred Morgans, Thorough-breds and Mustangs to produce a horse that would carry a rider at a steady speed over long distances and rough terrain. They later introduced Tennessee Walking Horse and Saddlebred blood to develop a horse with the unique dancing gait called the fox trot.

One of the most recent American additions to the equine world is the Rocky Mountain Horse. This breed's origins began in Kentucky with early Spanish imports and Mustang ponies. The founder, Sam Tuttle, owned a pre-potent stallion named Old Tobe. This stallion had a great disposition, was sure-footed and moved with a comfortable gait that was well suited to the hills of Appalachia. The Rocky Mountain Horse is relatively recent, and is not yet officially considered a "breed." The Rocky Mountain Horse Registry began in 1986, and today there are more than 200 horses registered.

This is not even the complete list of American-made horses. How many more can you name? The American Bashkir Curly Horse, the Florida Cracker Horse and the Thorcheron can also be added to the list, as well as many others. All unique, all special, all

Made in America!

C P M
T J W
F Y O
G V
I R N O L G R I P T B H T Z U R C I R O A U L O B B V A L
O Y C W L I D A M E R I C A N Q U A R T E R H O R S E A I
U N A M E R I C A N M A M M O T H J A C K S T O C K C I
L O S L M P L N W N T T R E M K M M E D H J P S N L F K
V P O N Y O F T H E A M E R I C A S S B M O R G A N J U L
I E O R H U M I S S O U R I F O X T R O T T E R M E B N Z
R U L V W L V A A S A I H C M T H N O V O S K V E Q I J
G G A X M T H A M E R I C A N B A S H K I R C U R L Y W
I A P Z O M S W E E A B Z N V O F T N P N E A N I R U X L
N E P R N F Z D R W L Q I C S P E A I D N G R J C I N Q E
I T A Q Z O N H I A E M J R Y Y W N A U H N C Y A C R W
A O P Q G P Z P C L W D Q E F W D D T H N A A E N S Q O
H C J K W B H K A K J U I M U S T A N G L R D C C A M O U
I N I W Z F N C N I D P L E K O O R U P W O I M R V T G B
G I R H U N B T S N E U H A U C V D O L Q D R B E R N C
H H A Q Y O O T H G Z S Z N R I C B M B H A O Z M A K I
L C R B G V X J E H D N L D S I T R Y N J R L K E N D Z R
A D I P C E L P T O C W G W E G I E K C T O F W D A X K D
N B C V U X N B L R Y L T H T N V D C G G L E H R Y K U
D E R B E L D D A S N A C I R E M A O Q G O R E A X F N
E V N E A V D J N E P Q T T I T F V R R T C M K F H I H S
R K Z P R D J W D D N O R E H C R O H T E S O X T J R G T
V T
A C
A B
L B

American Bashkir Curly
American Creme Draft
American Creme and White
American Mammoth Jackstock
American Quarter Horse
American Saddlebred
American Shetland
Appaloosa
Chincoteague Pony
Colorado Ranger
Florida Cracker
Missouri Fox Trotter
Morgan
Mustang
Pony of the Americas (POA)
Rocky Mountain Horse
Standardbred
Tennessee Walking Horse
Thorcheron
Virginia Highlander
Welara

Fight or Flight!

Wild horses are "prey" animals. This means other animals hunt them for food. These hunting animals are known as predators. How have horses avoided becoming another animal's dinner?

Living together in a herd, wild horses practice safety in numbers. Members of the herd take turns eating, drinking and resting, as other horses keep alert for danger. Horses have successfully adapted to their environment in many special ways:

- Horses have the largest eyes of any land mammal.
- Horses can sleep standing up.
- Horses have their eyes on each side of their head. (Think of a predator animal, like a wolf. Where are its eyes?)
- Horses can move their ears independently in different directions.
- Horses can run quickly and for long distances.

When danger is present, a horse has one of two choices. It can either stand and fight or run away. This is called the "fight or flight" response. Most of the time a horse will choose to escape the dangerous situation by running away. A horse usually only chooses to fight when it is cornered and has no way to escape.

The "fight or flight" response is a natural instinct that domestic horses still carry with them. By understanding how a horse reacts when it feels threatened or in danger, a rider can develop a trusting partnership with a horse.

Behavior

can you escape?

The Little Iron Horse

The Canadian Horse is a living tribute to the history of Canada. It is related to some of the very best horses of King Louis the 14th of France. King Louis sent horses to the French settlers in New France (Quebec) in the late 1600's. The horses he sent included a variety of breeds: Norman, Breton, Arab, Spanish Barb and Andalusian. For more than 150 years, these horses were interbred by French settlers with no outside influences. Over time, the unique Canadian Horse developed as a distinct breed.

This horse is known as "Cheval Canadien" to natives of Quebec, who still speak French today. The Canadian Horse survived and thrived under very difficult conditions. During the summer, the settlers had little use for their horses, so they ran loose in the woods. Because of the French practice of docking a horse's tail short, they had no defense against the flies. In winter, the horses had no shelter and survived mostly on straw and the little grain the hungry settlers could spare. The horses adapted to these harsh conditions over time, becoming smaller and sturdier. Today the Canadian Horse is recognized for being both strong and an easy keeper. These traits have earned it the nickname "The Little Iron Horse."

The typical Canadian Horse is around 15 hands, weighing between 1,000-1,400 pounds. Their strong legs, sturdy bones and excellent hooves are an important part of their "Iron Horse" reputation. Usually black, they can also be bay, brown or chestnut. Its full tail and mane is often wavy or curly. Canadian Horses are considered very sociable, intelligent and easy to train.

A little-known breed (even to many Canadians), the Canadian Horse contributed to the development of several North American breeds, including the Standardbred, American Saddlebred, Tennessee Walker and the Morgan.

Considered a rare breed today, the Canadian Horse was quite common in the mid-1800's, when they numbered more than 150,000. Many factors affected the breed population, including a large number of "Little Iron Horses" exported from Canada to the United States for stagecoach lines and the American Civil War. As farmers acquired tractors and trucks, the Canadian Horse was on the verge of extinction. By the mid-1970's, there were only 400 of these unique horses left.

When it appeared the breed might disappear altogether in the 1970's, a group of breeders dedicated to preserving "Cheval Canadien" began a special effort. There are nearly 2,200 registered Canadian Horses today. This breed is still considered an endangered species. While the majority of Canadian Horses are still found in Quebec, they are also found in smaller numbers in other Canadian provinces and with breeders in the United States.

The Canadian Horse is commonly used for driving, but is suitable for most other disciplines as well. Notice the trademark full and flowing mane and tail.

Whats in a name?

Canadian Horses have very long registered names. You can tell a lot about a horse from just his or her name. An official registered Canadian Horse name contains three parts:
the herd name, the sire's name, and the horse's individual name (starting with the letter assigned to the year of its birth by the breed registry, 1995=E, 1996=F, 1997=G, etc.). Sound confusing? Here is an example:

Hidden Meadow Star Gambit - Hidden Meadow Farm owned the dam (mother)
at the time of the foal's birth. The stallion Rainville Wilifred Star sired the foal.
The foal was born in 1997 because the individual name begins with the letter G.

You can visit Hidden Meadow Farm online at http://www.canadianhorses.com

cross

'his breed got its name from the "standard" acing time required to enter the stud book. (12)
'rench for "Canadian Horse." (6,8)
'his breed is famous for its running walk. (9,6)
'his breed was named for its schoolmaster wner. (6)
Canadian Horse's individual name begins with he ________ assigned to the year of its birth. (6)

own

'he nickname for the Canadian Horse. (6,4,5)
Iorses were sent from this country to Canada y the King. (6)
'he most common color for the Canadien Horse. (5)
term that describes a horse that requires little extra eed or special care. (4,6)
'he province in Canada where most Canadian Horses re found. (6)
'he most common use of the Canadian Horse. (7)
'his horse measurement equals four inches. (4)

The Equine Heavyweights

It's a good thing draft horses are known for their good disposition. They can stand as tall as 18 hands high (6 feet) at the withers and can weigh as more than one ton (2,000 pounds).

These great horses were used to carry heavily armored knights into battle during the Middle Ages. Up until the early and mid 1900's, heavy horses were used for pulling wagons, plowing and logging.

The most well known draft horses today are probably the flashy Clydesdale teams used to pull wagons for Budweiser Brewing Corp. Draft horses are making a comeback in the United States and can be seen up close and personal at most county fairs.

Also called the cold-blooded breeds (Arabs and Thoroughbreds are considered hot-blooded), draft horses typically have short strong backs; short legs as compared to their height; broad, powerful chests; gentle dispositions and enormous strength. Some draft breeds grow long fine hair around their lower legs, called feathers. Clydesdales, Shires and Belgians all have feathers.

Over the centuries, draft horses crossed with hot-blooded horses have resulted in a group of distinct breeds known as warmbloods. The Dutch Warmblood, Westphalian, Trakehner, Hanoverian, Oldenburg and Holsteiner are all distinct warmblood breeds that owe much of their power and stamina to the draft horse.

Draft horses were used in medieval England to carry a knight in full armor. The knight mounted his horse just before battle. The rest of the time it was led from the right by his squire. A war horse became known as a Destrier, from the Latin word "dextrarius," meaning the right side.

Draft horses once supplied the "real horsepower" that trucks and tractors do today.

aft horses are
o called
old-blooded"
eeds. They
descended
m the pre-
storic Forest
orse.

X

O H W

Y S R O X

V V U Y V D J

R L W F D G Q W M

J U A R F H K N X X E

H C S D E O Z Y F K O N Q

K O T S M Z L F E T T B F I C

F U E X I I O K J R L F F R G V U

I A J P O A R K P M S I A N N E D R A

U Y U E E V N H A U T F A R D H C T U D Z

V E K N O R T H E R N S W E D I S H H O R S E

U C X W T H C L E A U C E T Y Y M G E J G N R B Y

I D O X I D Z H T A V M H Z J N V U D G D X M R S U W

K B J L G M E C V Y F T C X O A I N S E Y A T U E

L J X L V R C Y D P S H I R E N I J W B L M B

W C N C O H D R D F V D M H A N X A D C C

X O I N B R A F H H P A N O G N Z L H

Q M V G A F V S U D N A L T U J S

Q T E F T I Q Q A C I P P U R

I O T R K R L H O L O G G

M I I R U J F B A P B

K S O H J N N T C

B I P M K W I

U H O P T

T X E

A

re is the largest horse breed
world. Shires average 17
igh and weigh more than
ounds.

Ardennais (France)
Boulannais (France)
Brabant (Belgium)
Breton (France)
Clydesdale (Scotland)
Comtois (France)
Dutch Draft (Holland)
Irish Draught (Ireland)
Italian Heavy Draft (Italy)
Jutland (Denmark)
Murakozer (Hungary)
Norman Cob (France)
Northern Swedish Horse (Sweden)
Percheron (France)
Poitevin (France)
Russian Heavy Draft (Ukraine)
Shire (England)
Suffolk Punch (England)
Vladmir Heavy Draft (Russia)

Brooklyn Supreme, a Belgian horse who lived in Iowa between 1928-1948, holds the record as the world's largest horse. He stood 19.2 hands high and weighed 3,200 pounds!

The Love of Ponies

The official definition of a pony is "any horse that measures 14.2 hands (58 inches) or less at the withers." A more fitting definition might be "an amazing equine in a small package that touches the heart of nearly everyone he meets."

Pound per pound, ponies have amazing strength in relation to their small size. In general, most ponies have sturdy, compact bodies. They are very hardy and healthy, able to survive and thrive in harsh environments. Ponies can live a long time. It is not unusual for ponies to be healthy and active at age 30 or more.

Ponies come in all colors, shapes and sizes. Most ponies carry long thick manes and tails, adding to their special beauty. The Hafflinger is one of the few pony breeds that does not display the typical equine coat colors. Instead, Hafflingers are nearly always a variation of chestnut with a long flaxen mane and tail.

There are many unique pony breeds found in locations around the world. Over the centuries, these different breeds have adapted to be successful in their specific habitat. For example, the Dartmoor Pony is small and stocky with a thick coat to help survive the cold climate of northern Europe. The Shetland Pony developed on the rocky Shetland Isles, and in comparison to their small size, are considered the most powerful equine in the world. Both the Shetland and the Dartmoor still display the large nostrils and nasal cavities for warming the air before it enters the lungs, typical of ponies that developed in the colder northern European climate. In comparison, the Java Pony is a much lighter pony, used today to pull two-wheeled taxis in Indonesia. It descended from the Mongolian Wild Horse and has adapted over the centuries to withstand the tropical heat and humidity.

Whatever their color, shape or size, one thing is certain. Ponies are loved around the world!

The Manipur developed in India
many centuries, a combination o
Mongolian Wild Horse and Ara
blood. It was the original polo p
dating back nearly 1300 years.

caspian

The rare Caspian is considered t
most ancient equine breed, and
haps an ancestor of the Arabian.
descended from the wild native
of Iran. There are less than 450
registered purebreds today.

shetland

The Noma is the smallest native pony of Japan, standing only 10.1 hands. There are less than 40 known purebred Nomas today. They are being preserved as part of Japan's cultural heritage.

exmoor

Breeds

The Connemara is the only equine breed to develop in Ireland. They are famous for being fast, brave, sensible and amazing jumpers.

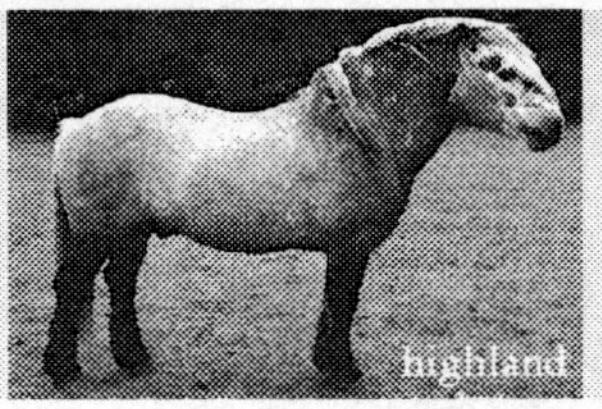
highland

Queen Elizabeth of England breeds Highland ponies at her Balmoral Estate in Scotland. She rides one of her Highland ponies nearly every day on her summer visits.

basotho

e Java Pony
eloped on
island of
a from the
ngolian
ld Horse.
er the cen-
ies they have
pted
the tropical
t, pulling
-wheeled
s all day
hout tiring.

```
J Q A P Y X X G Z W M N Q T T X B K E L H X J E L
Y G U O H Q J Z C G L G Q V E D N A L T E H S F F
F D A V M B I P Q U D A R T M O O R O A H U A H Y
U M C I C D F H C I D R P E O L R X U I G Z C O P
S K R O S S S U R G O K S B L G W H O S L N S A K
L X E C Q C H I N C O T E A G U E N A N K P E M G
Z N M G E X M O O R E H U M V D G C R I O L L O B
V P Y L W B N C H E J U U Q I B I V Q E J P N N T
J R A E E E R C V T G A U S T R A L I A N A E Q I
Y C N C N W U C F C O E G W E A N M V M I W W R U
R C G X A K K F T N E S I M W N F A L G F X F M A
X W R N T C C O N N E M A R A D J I I O Y E O M A
Q E I U B D N A L S I E L B A S O D U R T S R N I
A L I N T A I S H U H C L L O D R N A Z M U E I L
I T J J I P Q K Y T M I E C V A D E E H B T S W Y
F O C L S Z H M F Z H S F L B L O E G C D Y T A A
G W P A B K C O T T O P L N A H J M A N I P U R B
K P C Q L O Y Z L B Q D G N L N S X A X I L A Q G
I J D U T N T I W S K H D S E R D L A Z B L A C O
C V H S O I X V K B S A I I A Z H I E Z E V F G H
P A X P J K I O H T I O R K R G S I C W S E U A R
H K N S J V H X S S U X P T I O T O G W V B I A H
H X E J M E S M N A V J N H C E Q R R U O Y H Z T
S P P V P G E B T A X D Q K C U K R K L C T G Q X
N K E Y Z J B I H Q R M Z F T J T A L C L H S A E
```

The small but hardy Cheju is in serious risk of extinction. In 1987, the Korean government designated the Cheju a national treasure to help preserve the breed.

Ariegeois (Spain)
Australian (Australia)
Balearic (Spain - Isle of Majorca)
Bardigiano (Italy)
Basotho (South Africa)
Basuto (South Africa)
Burma (Burma)
Caspian (Iran)
Cheju (Korea)
Chincoteague (USA)
Connemara (Ireland)
Criollo (Argentina)
Dales (England)
Dartmoor (England)
Dol Gudbrandsdal (Norway)
Exmoor (England)
Fell (England)
Galiceno (Mexico)
Hackney (England)
Haflinger (Austria)
Highland (Scotland)
Hucul (Poland)
Icelandic (Iceland)
Java (Indonesia)
Konik (Poland)
Landais (France)
Manipur (India)
New Forest (England)
Newfoundland (Newfoundland)
Noma (Japan)
Pony of the Americas (USA)
Pottock (France)
Sable Island (Nova Scotia)
Shetland (Scotland-Shetland Isles)
Skogruss (Sweden)
Taishuh (Japan)
Welara (USA)
Welsh (Wales)

sotho is used only for
in South Africa.
are used for plowing
uling.) In addition to
lk, trot and canter, this
as two additonal gaits:
pple and the pace.

icelandic

Pumpkin, a miniature
oaled in South Carolina
3, measured 14 inches
withers and weighed
nds at age 2.

welsh

Developing as a unique breed in Mexico, the Galiceno has Spanish ancestry. It is famous for its swift and smooth "running walk."

The Norwegian Fjord

Let It Snow! Norwegian Fjord stallion Hostar exhibits all of the classic color, conformation, ath ability and disposition for which the breed is famous. Driven here by Craig Wich, he is owned & Laura Wich of Mink Hollow Fjords in Thetford Center, Vermont. You can view the Mink Hollo website to learn more about Fjords and check out his photo album of foals at www.norwegian

Not only did Vikings sail ships on the sea, they made war on land astride sturdy dun horses. Rare and wonderful, the Norwegian Fjord horse is now gaining popularity in the United States. Pronounced "fee-ord," it is Norway's oldest horse breed. Scientists believe that the ancestors of the Fjord migrated to Norway over 4,000 years ago. They were domesticated about 2,000 years ago and used as war mounts and for farming.

The Norwegian Fjord is one of the few modern horse breeds to exhibit only the primitive dun color and markings. Each Fjord has a dark dorsal stripe that begins at the base of the forelock, running through the center of the mane, down the back and to the tail. Fjords also have dark points on their legs and leg bars that resemble zebra stripes. Look up the Przewalski Wild Horse in Central Asia and you will see why scientists believe that the Fjord is one of the few horse breeds that kept their original wild color characteristics.

These sturdy horses are well-known for their intelligence, mild manners and dependability. Fjords have been selectively bred in Norway since the 1880's. To help preserve this national treasure, all breeding in Norway is controlled by a government agency. Only champion Fjord stock is permitted to be exported from Norway.

The modern Fjord is a very square and compact animal with a powerful neck. Their short but sturdy legs make them sure-footed in the roughest terrain. Because of the Fjord's agility and surefootedness, this breed of horse is highly prized by the military. Fjords can go where motorized vehicles and other horses must give up. Internationally, the Fjord is recognized as the best mountain army horse in the world. Fjords are also valued for being "easy keepers," usually thriving on hay alone.

The Fjord averages 13.2 to 15 hands tall, averaging from 1,000 - 1,400 pounds. They are strong enough to carry an adult and their excellent disposition also makes them an ideal driving animal. Used for farming in Europe for centuries, it is believed that many of the present-day draft breeds are related in some way to the Fjord. The gait of the "Fjording," as they are referred to in daily Norwegian speech, is smooth with a trot that easily covers mile after mile.

Fjords were first imported into the United States in the 1950's and 1960's. Their popularity continues to grow, mainly because of their wonderful disposition. Their versatility has helped them become an ideal family horse. They are used for both English and Western riding, jumping, dressage and driving. People who purchase their first Fjord as a novelty often become hooked on these Norwegian wonder-horses. To learn more about the Norwegian Fjord contact:

Norwegian Fjord Association
of North America
24570 W. Chardon Rd.
Grayslake, IL 60030.
Phone: 708-546-7881

Across

1 The Fjord's great ____________ is a major factor in the breed's success and popularity. (11)

3 The Norwegian word for the Fjord. (8)

5 Another word for agriculture. (7)

10 A wild animal that has been tamed to live and work with humans. (12)

11 This country has the Fjord as its national horse. (6)

12 How the early ancestors of the Fjord got to Norway. (8)

Down

1 This dark stripe runs along a dun horse's spine. (6)

2 The __________ breed of horse in Norway. (6)

4 These ancient warriors rode the sturdy Fjord in battle. (7)

6 The only truly wild horse, found today in Central Asia. (10)

7 A term to describe a horse that does not require special feeds or care. (4,6)

8 Only this quality of Fjord can be exported to another country. (8)

9 These leg markings look like zebra stripes. (7)

10 Considered a primitive horse coloring, seen today in the Fjord and Przewalski. (3)

The American Bashkir Curly Horse

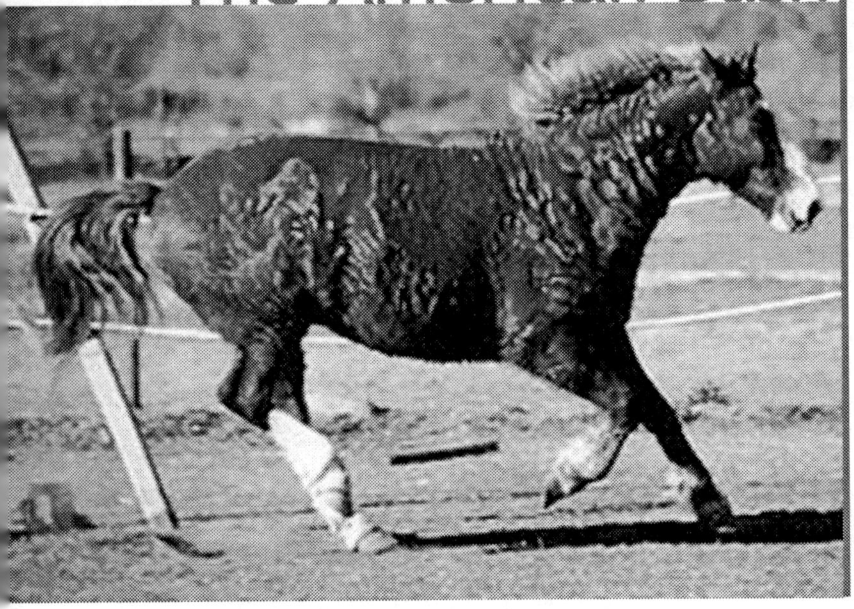

Have you ever seen a horse with a curly coat and mane? The exact origin of the Curly horse remains one of the mysteries of the equine world. It is known that Curly horses are an ancient breed. Horses with curly coats have been depicted in Chinese art and statues as far back as 161 A.D. When Napoleon invaded Austria in 1805, he discovered six "poodle horses" at the Vienna Zoo and took some of them with him when he returned to France. The Native American Sioux drew pictographs of curly-coated horses for their "Winter Count" in 1802, illustrating some horses they had stolen from the Crow tribes. P.T. Barnum exhibited a curly-coated horse in his museum from 1843-1848, before he started his travelling circus. Chief Red Cloud even mentioned a brave on a curly horse at the Battle of Little Bighorn.

The history of the American Bashkir Curly can be more clearly traced. It dates back to 1898, when a young boy named Peter Damele and his father were riding through the Peter Hanson mountain range in the remote high country of central Nevada. They came upon a herd of sturdy, curly-coated wild horses. Where these horses originated remains a mystery. The Damele family bred and used Curly horses on their ranch for almost 100 years. Peter's late son Benny continued to breed them for ranch work until 1992. Many of the American Bashkir Curlies registered today can be traced back to the Damele herd.

The American Bashkir Curly is found in all common horse colors. They are medium-sized with many breed characteristics in addition to heavy winter coats made up of kinky, corkscrew curls. The face of a Curly shows gentle wide-set eyes, thought to give them a wider range of vision. Many Curlies have no ergot, the small bony patch usually found behind the fetlock. Scientists have also discovered that Curly horses have an unusually high concentration of red blood cells, which may be one reason why they are such a hardy and healthy breed.

In recent years, the Curly horse has been used for pleasure, gymkhana, roping, endurance riding, dressage and driving.

The American Bashkir Curly Registry was established in 1971 by a small group of breeders with a deep love for these special horses. Their sole purpose is to preserve and promote the curly-coated horse. To learn more about these horses, write to:

The American Bashkir Curly Registry
P.O. Box 264
Ely, Nevada 89301

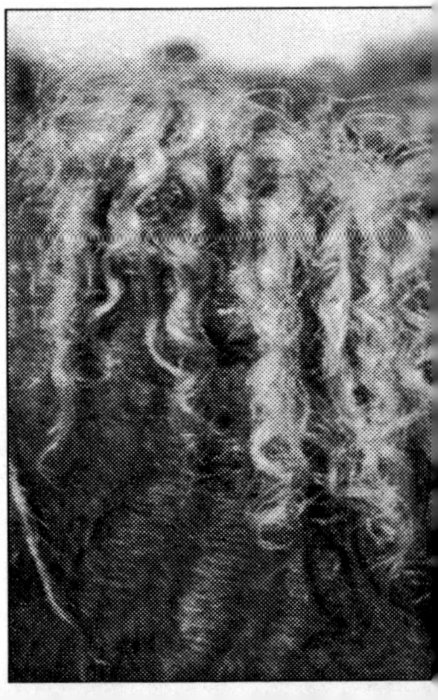

Curlies have a fine soft mane that splits in the middle into tight curly ringlets. It is not uncommon for Curlies to completely shed their mane each spring along with their winter coat.

Across

2 This area goes from behind the shoulder to the flank. (6)

6 The hard bony patch behind the fetlock. (5)

7 This bone is found between theknee and the fetlock in the front leg and between the hock and the fetlock on the hind leg. (6)

9 This French emperor conquered much of Europe in the early 1800's. (8)

10 In this state, the first documented sighting of the horse that is today known as the American Bashkir Curly. (6)

12 The joint between the cannon bone and the pastern. (7)

15 An organization that preserves and promotes an individual breed. (5,8)

16 The six horses at the Vienna Zoo in 1805 were called ___________ .

Down

1 This dark spot on a horse's coat was highly prized by Native Americans. (8,4)

3 Curly horses are well-suited for this kind of work, which they performed for the Damele family. (5)

4 A high concentration of these is thought to make Curlies hardy and healthy. (3,5,5)

5 This famous circus promoter once owned a curly-coated horse. (2,6)

7 Horses with curly coats were used in the ancient art of this country. (5)

8 This family raised Curly horses foralmost 100 years. (6)

11 The spinal column is made up of these small bones. (9)

13 Curlies often shed this along with their winter coat. (4)

14 Horses living wild that were domesticated at one time. (5)

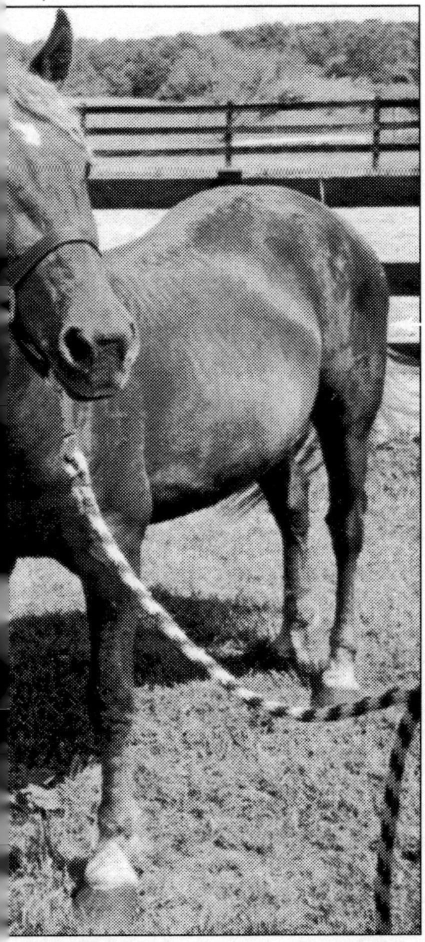

medicine mark

This is Kayla, a three year old registered American Bashkir Curly. She is owned by Linda Stermer of Lawrence, Michigan. Kayla was originally part of a herd of feral horses in North Dakota. Like most Curlies, Kayla has tough black hooves, stout round cannon bones, straight legs and flat knees. Most Curlies have a short back with only five lumbar vertebrae and a round rump without a crease. Other breed characteristics include powerful rounded shoulders, a "V" chest and a round barrel. They often have "curly" eyelashes and curls inside their ears. Notice the dark spot on Kayla's right hip, referred to as a "medicine mark." A horse with a medicine mark was highly prized by Native Americans.

Marguerite Henry's Misty of Chincoteague Oat Cake

Ingredients:

- 2 1/4 cups flour
- 1 1/2 cups sugar
- 3 teaspoons baking powder
- 1 teaspoon salt
- 1 cup oats
- 1/2 cup shortening
- 2 egg yolks
- 2 egg whites
- 1 cup milk
- 1/4 cup finely chopped walnuts
- molasses

Preheat oven to 350°. Grease and flour two 9-inch layer cake pans. Sift together: flour, sugar, baking powder and salt. Mix in oats. Add shortening. Beat egg yolks and milk. After well mixed, fold in egg whites.

Bake at 350° for 35 to 40 minutes. Test with a toothpick. When cool, spread top with molasses and sprinkle with walnuts. For horses and people, too!

Majesty's Mellowcreme Treats

Here's a fun dessert for any season!

Ingredients:

- 2 tablespoons margarine
- 20 marshmallows
- 2 cups sweet feed
- 1 cup cracked corn
  (or you may substitute with all sweet feed or all oats)
- 1/2 cup mellowcreme treats
  (such as candy corn, pumpkins, santas, etc.)
- 1/2 cup bran

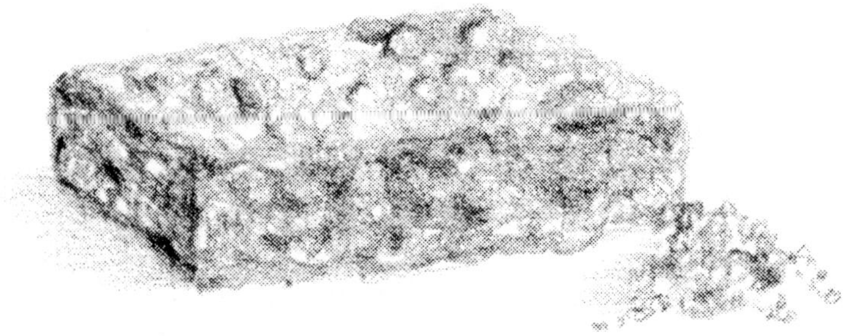

Lightly grease with margarine an 8 x 8 cake pan and dust with bran. Set aside.

Melt margarine in a 4-quart saucepan over medium heat. Add marshmallows gradually, stirring constantly until melted. Remove from heat and add sweet feed, cracked corn and candy (candy corn, pumpkins, etc.). Stir well until coated. Transfer into the cake pan, dust top with bran and press down. Cool and cut into squares. Dust with more bran.

Recipes reprinted with permission from ***The Original Book of Horse Treats*** by June V. Evers.
See page 64 to order the book.

Get Busy With Beads!

You can create hat bands, key chains, necklaces and more using this simple technique...

Items needed:

- pony beads (large hole)
- leather lacing or cord

Optional items:

- conchas
- bells
- keyrings

Start with two equal lengths of lace or cord. Start with longer lengths of cord than what the finished product will be. Estimate approximately $1^{1}/_{2}$ times the desired finished length.

Put both pieces through a single bead.

Separate the two laces and string 4-5 beads on each one.

Join the two laces together by stringing them through a single bead.

Repeat the pattern, varying the number of beads every other section.

When it reaches the desired length, thread both ends (all 4 laces) through a concha or larger bead.

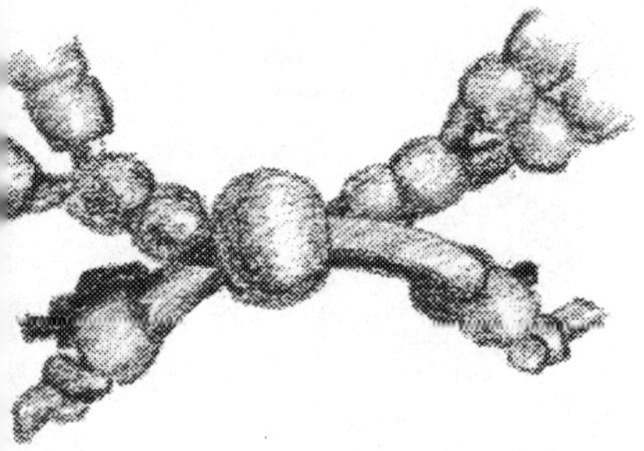

Your choices are endless — key chains, hat bands, boot bracelets, necklaces, belts...

All In the Family

Horses, asses and zebras all belong to a family of mammals called ***Equidae***. In the wild, equids feed by grazing on grasses, live in open country and escape predators by running swiftly. Equids are also highly social, living in herds that consist of many family groups.

Domestic horses still have many of these needs and instincts. These are important factors to keep in mind in the care for and training of your own horse.

All equids are closely related genetically and can interbreed, although the resulting offspring are usually sterile and cannot reproduce themselves. Here are some examples:

male donkey + female horse =	Mule
female donkey + male horse =	Hinny
zebra + horse =	Zebroid
zebra + donkey =	Zedonk

Most Americans don't know that George Washington was a mule breeder. His goal was to produce large mules for draft work. At that time, most of the donkeys in North America were not big or strong enough to sire this kind of mule. The best donkeys were in Spain, but they were not permitted to be exported to other countries. Washington wrote to the King of Spain personally, to ask about purchasing some good quality donkeys for breeding stock. The King sent Washington two jacks (male donkeys) and two jennets (female donkeys) as a gift in 1785. One of the jacks died during the long voyage, but the surviving jack was named Royal Gift. Later the Marquis de Lafayette sent Washington a black Maltese jack and several jennets. Crossbred with Washington's Andalusians, this became the foundation stock for the breed known today as the American Mammoth Mule. Although their numbers are increasing, this breed is still considered endangered. Their numbers **are estimated to be less than 2,500 worldwide.**

chariot racing

jumping

4-up wagon

dressage

From racing to packing, jumping, reining, driving, pleasure riding, the mules at Bishop Mule Days compete in a variety of events. And many times, the mules in the pleasure classes later appear on the race track, under harness or in a packstring.

packing

Patchwork Paint Patterns

Tobiano: (toe-bee-ah-no) The white areas usually have a distinct, sharp edge to them. The topline is usually crossed at some point by a white patch. A Tobiano can range from very little white spotting to a horse largely white (most often, a white body and a colored head). Tobiano spotting is arranged vertically.

Tobiano Characteristics

1. White will cross the back between the withers and the dock of the tail.
2. Generally all four of the tobiano's legs are white, at least below the hocks and knees.
3. They will have face markings of a normal horse, such as a star, snip, stripe, blaze, or no marking at all on the face.
4. The spots are rounded or oval shapes and generally the dark color will extend down the neck, giving the appearence of a shield. It is typical for the dark color to cover at least one of the flank areas.
5. The tail often has two colors.
6. Tobiano horses can be predominantly dark or white in appearance.

Overo: (oh-vah-roh) White areas display a ragged edge and it is rare for the white to extend onto the topline. The white body patches commonly occur in the middle of the sides and neck and sometimes appearing on the belly. Overo spotting is arranged horizonally.

Overo Characteristics

1. Generally white will not cross the back between the withers and the dock of the tail.
2. An overo may either have no white markings on their legs or extremely high white socks.
3. Overo horses generally have white markings on their faces. Usually there is a blaze or more. This would also include apron or bonnet face markings.
4. The horse tail is generally one color.
5. The overo markings are generally scattered and irregular.
6. Overos can be either predominantly dark or white.

C

O T

D

O T

E

O T

Lethal White: A foal of overo lineage, born all white or mostly white. The foal may seem normal at birth, but usually begins showing signs of colic within 12 hours because of a non-functioning colon. Because the syndrome is always fatal, lethal white foals are often euthanized.

Tovero: (toe-vah-roh) White areas will display patterns of both the Tobiano and Overo. The Tovero may display an Overo pattern head with body pattern of a Tobiano (sometimes this pattern is hard to distinguish because it is very subtle).

Sabino: (sah-bee-no) - a distinct pattern and sometimes called a "Flecked Roan". The white patches are quite variable. On some horses they are very sharp and distinct, while others may only have a flecking of small spots of white on the background color. The pattern is usually much more ragged and irregular and the flecks, roaning and white patches are more evident than that of an Overo pattern. Most Sabinos have a "bald" or "apron" face.

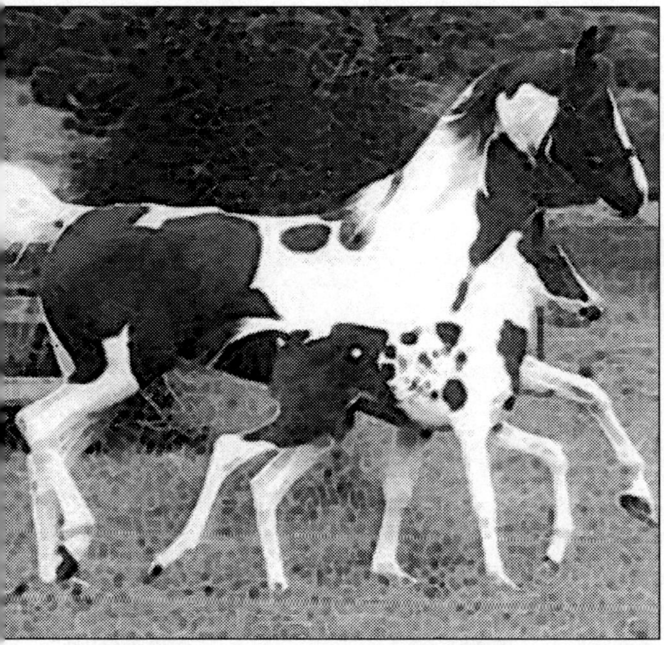

Rabicano: (rah-bee-cah-no) This pattern of white hairs seems to extend out from the flank as well as numberous white hairs at the base of the tail. Extensively marked horses are confused with "roans," but Rabicano roaning does not cover the whole body.

For more information, visit APHA at http://www.apha.com

Which Pattern?

Tobiano or Overo (no mixtures here).

F ☐

O T

G ☐

O T

Facial Markings

The size and shape of facial marking are a useful additional way of describing and identifying an individual horse. These markings are recorded on veterinary certificates, breed registration papers and other documents.

Facial markings are drawn on the document, as well as a written description.

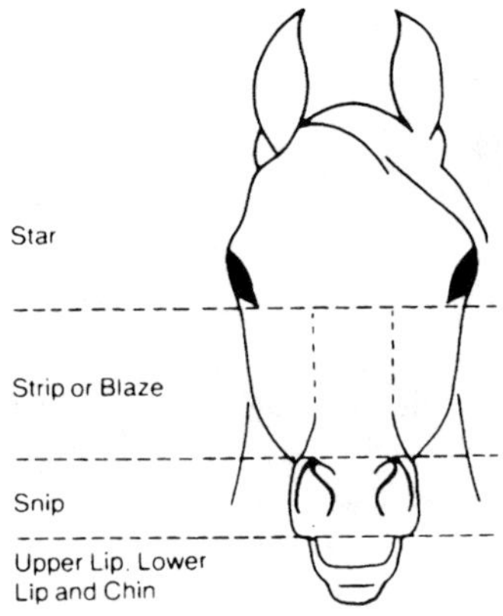

Blue eyes are common when a horse has a lot of white on its face.

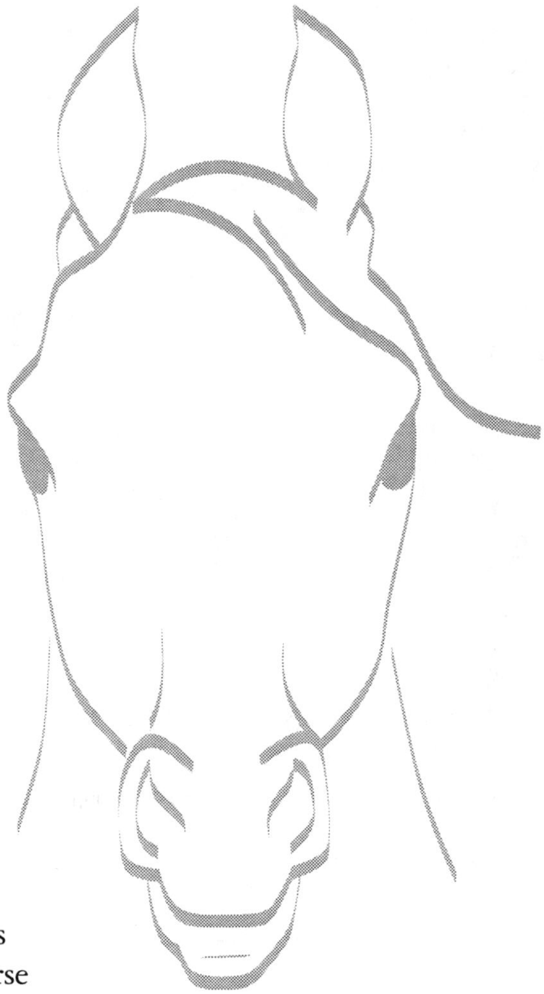

Draw the markings of your favorite horse (real or imaginary).

Match the marking to its name.

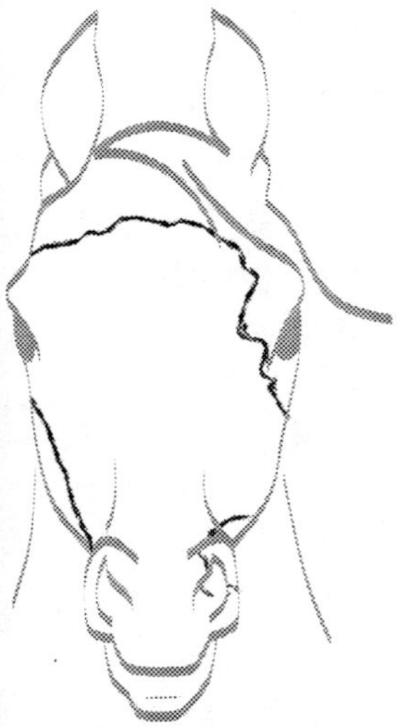

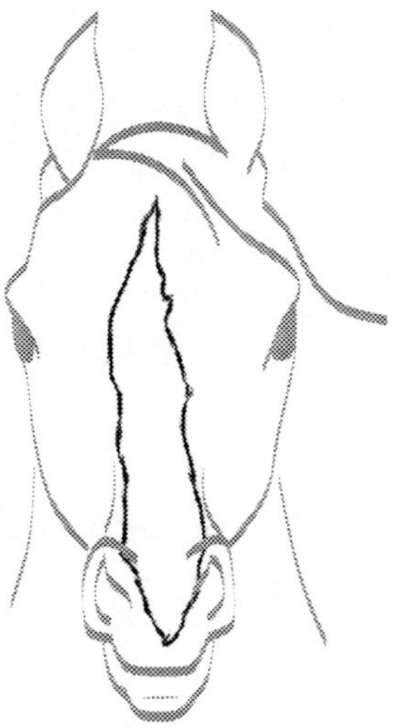

Snip

Stripe

Blaze

Star

Bald Face

Star/Stripe

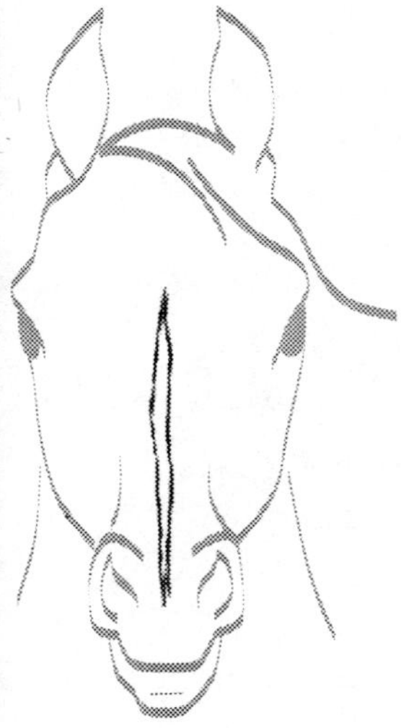

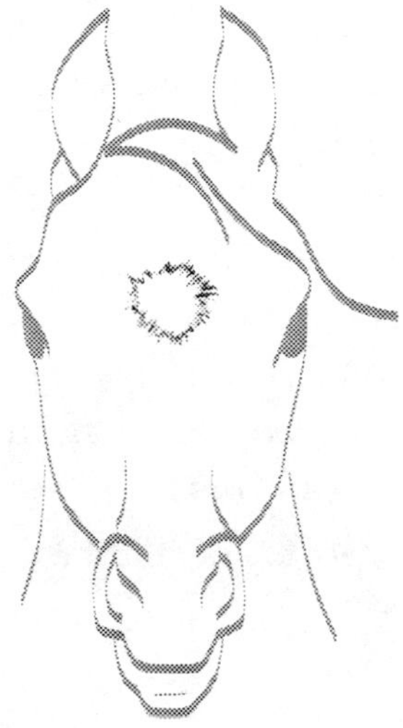

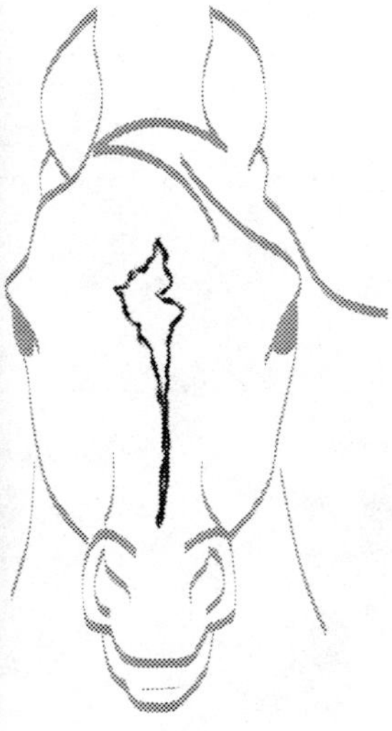

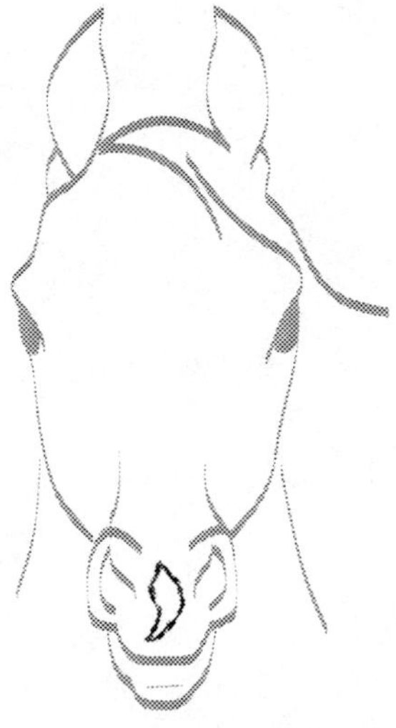

Just "Foaling" Around

Spring brings new babies to the animal kingdom, including the equine world. Will it be a boy (colt) or a girl (filly)? When will it arrive? What color will it be?

Patient mare owners have been waiting almost eleven months for their new arrival. Eleven months is the average length of a mare's pregnancy, which is called the "gestation period." That's about two months longer than our mothers had to wait before we were born!

When her time comes, a mare usually lies down to give birth. Twins are very rare for horses, so only one foal is expected. The birth process normally takes a few hours after her water breaks. When the foal is born, it usually arrives with its front feet presented first. The head and rest of the body follow. Unlike puppies and kittens, a baby horse is born with his eyes wide open. Soon after the foal is born, the mare gets up and licks her new baby clean. This also helps the foal's breathing and circulation.

After only an hour or so, the newborn foal is able to stand on long wobbly legs to nurse. This first milk is called "colostrum." It is very important for the foal to nurse in the first few hours after birth. Colostrum contains important antibodies to help the foal resist diseases, especially those that cause diarrhea and pneumonia.

After four to six hours, a newborn foal is able to walk and run alongside his mother. This is an important survival ability that helped wild horses escape hungry predators. How old were you before you could walk and run?

The colt or filly lives on mother's milk for about the first two months. Gradually the foal learns to graze on grass, just like mom. Foals are usually weaned from their mother's milk around six months of age.

If you are lucky enough to own or meet a foal this spring, don't blink! Foals grow quickly and reach half their adult size by the time they are one year old.

Reference: ***The Visual Dictionary of the Horse, Dorling Kindersley Publishing, 1994.***

Foals come in many colors. How many horse colors can you find?

```
F
S V B
I F Z
K I V V M
G F A H W
C S J H H P U
T M T Q X B O
F P P N E W N E U
W V V P W I A Y D
B I K L Q B O O X C X
R I H Y L P N R R K L
R J G R A L V I E B G P Z
K M H L R S T M U T I O R
C Z B L E G K E O L E T Q O L
H D E T E K N A L B N C I M E
T P U R A U R Z F A I I Y J B Z N
X R N F I E Z R L P L V A D F A H
E G Y R I R G B D O J E E E N O E E I
T H M D Z O C F V X S O L E R O T N L
S A C F M C Y S E H R T P X Y T C I S D F
B U I K N W A R B S U P A R A S K H K T X
V Y W F I G Q O I N R A L R U B S U W E P X H
B D V C C P E O E R D F E D H K A C L W S G A
K S S W Q Z F J E E H T B F O C C D W P B V T M B
Y J N O U V X Y J W Q W L T U O A B O L A S V N C
X C O V O T D N F L V A N R B S S L P P T L L U K U T
O E N E A O H Q C M R G Q S W B D B A U N D J E V Y T
U V G G F D R F U B T L C B Q H I K W Q E M N U Y R G A C
S X W Z H Y S O I S Y W T U O K M P D T H J V D X Q L V L
```

albino
bay
black
black bay
blanketed
blue roan
brown
buckskin
chestnut
creme
dappled
dun
flaxen
fleabitten
gray
gruella
leopard
liver chestnut
overo
palomino
piebald
pinto
skewbald
sorrel
strawberry roan
tobiano
white

What is Imprinting?

Imprinting is the learning process for a newborn foal. The imprinting and bonding period happens in the first few hours after birth. During this time a foal bonds closely with its mother. In the wild, a foal bonds with other members of the herd. A foal can also bond with other animals. When a domesticated horse is born, it can bond with humans that are present at birth. Imprinting at this young age can shape a horse's lifetime behavior.

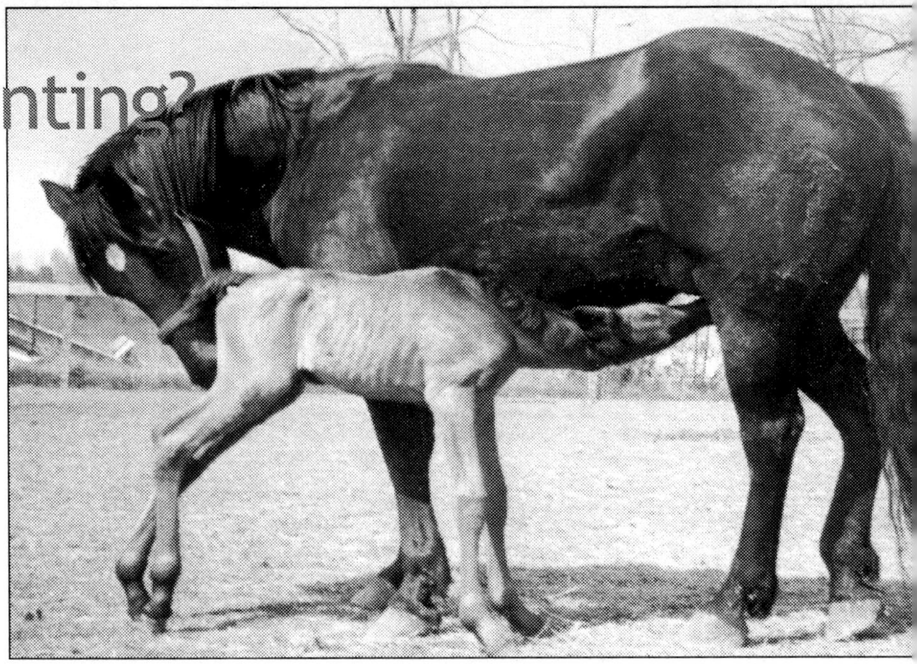

April Sonata and her new colt Andanté

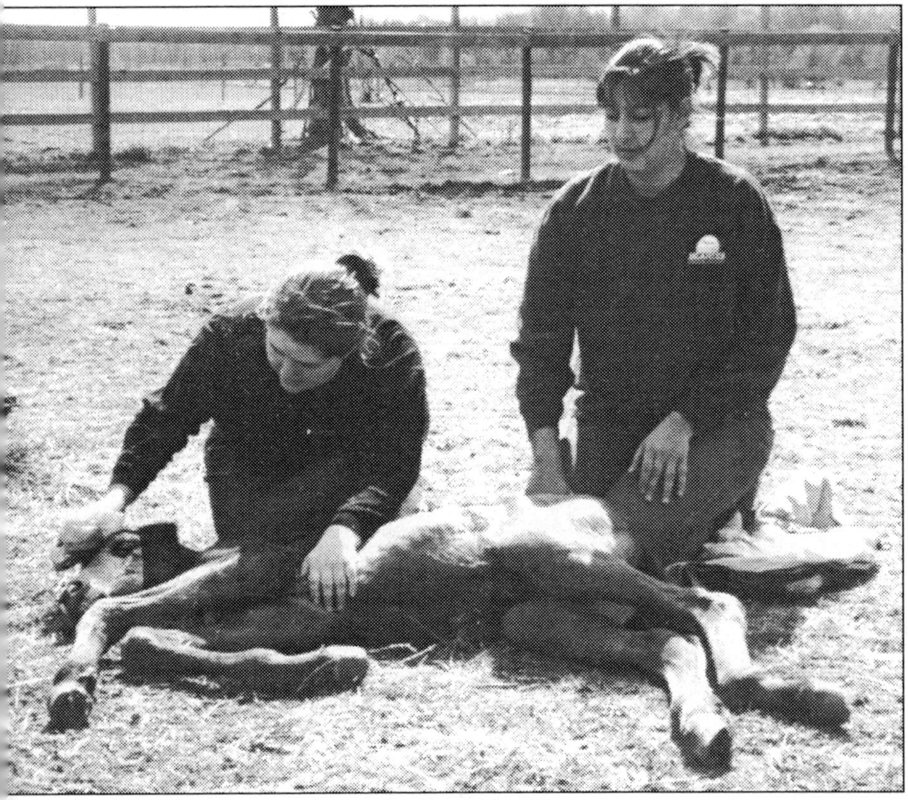

Andanté is only two hours old in this photo. The girls began the imprinting process after he had bonded with his mother and nursed for the first time. Newborn foals lay down often for naps, so it easy to continue short imprinting sessions in the hours following birth.

Why imprint a foal?

Domestic horses spend their entire lives living and working with humans. During training, humans often place horses in situations that are not natural conditions in the wild (for example, wearing horseshoes, riding in a horse trailer, carrying a rider). Spending time imprinting a newborn foal introduces a foal to things they will encounter in their life as a domestic horse.

Zzzzzzzzz.....

Imprinting Benefits:

Imprint trained foals tend to be more friendly and approachable, even when in pasture.

A newborn foal can be introduced to things like a human's touch, the spray of a fly spray bottle, the noise and vibration of electric clippers, etc. A foal should also become used to having its ears and teeth examined, hooves handled and other routine grooming and health care procedures.

Wild horses live in herds. Each herd has its own order of dominance. Domestic horses also live with a herd-based social system. A properly trained domestic horse must respect humans and accept human leadership, and obey our wishes. Since horses physically dominate humans with their size and strength, it is important to establish this dominance at a young age.

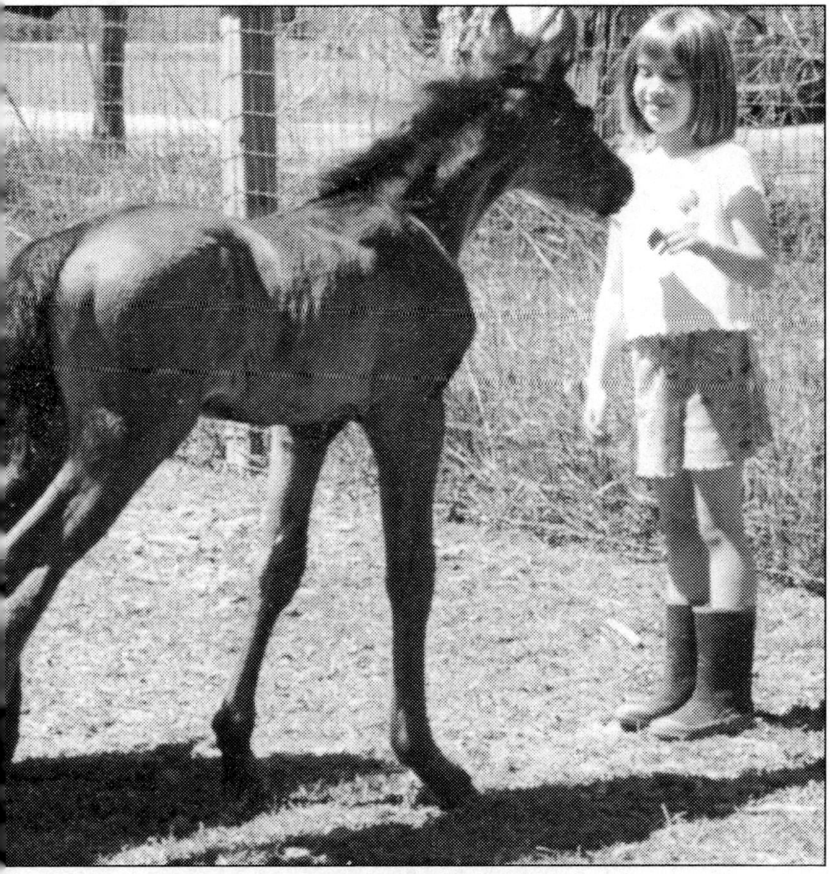

At only one week old, Andanté is friendly and approachable. He confidently steps away from his mother to greet a human member of his "herd." "After I petted him, Andanté tried to nibble the flowers on my t-shirt," said 8 year old Ali.

Learn more about imprinting

Imprint Training of the Newborn Foal
by Robert M. Miller, D.V.M.
Published by Western Horseman Inc., 1991.
(Now in its eleventh printing)

The Big C: COLIC!

Colic is not a disease. It is the name given to a physical symptom — abdominal pain. Preventing colic, recognizing the early warning signs of colic and treating colic are life-saving horsemanship skills. Colic is the number one cause of death in horses. Quickly recognizing the symptoms of colic and seeking veterinary help will greatly improve a horse's chance of recovery.

What does colic look like? Signs of colic can vary between individual horses. That's why it's important for you to know what is "normal" for your horse. Colic symptoms also vary depending upon how much pain the horse is experiencing.

The most common signs of colic include:

- turning the head toward the flank
- pawing
- kicking or biting the abdomen
- stretching out as if to urinate, without doing so
- repeatedly lying down and getting up (or attempting to do so)
- rolling, especially violent rolling
- sitting in a dog-like position, or lying on the back
- lack of appetite
- putting head down to water without drinking
- lack of bowel movements
- reduced or no gut (digestive) sounds
- sweating
- rapid breathing/flared nostrils
- elevated pulse (greater than 44 beats per minute)
- depression
- lip curling (Flehmen response)
- cool extremities (example: ears)

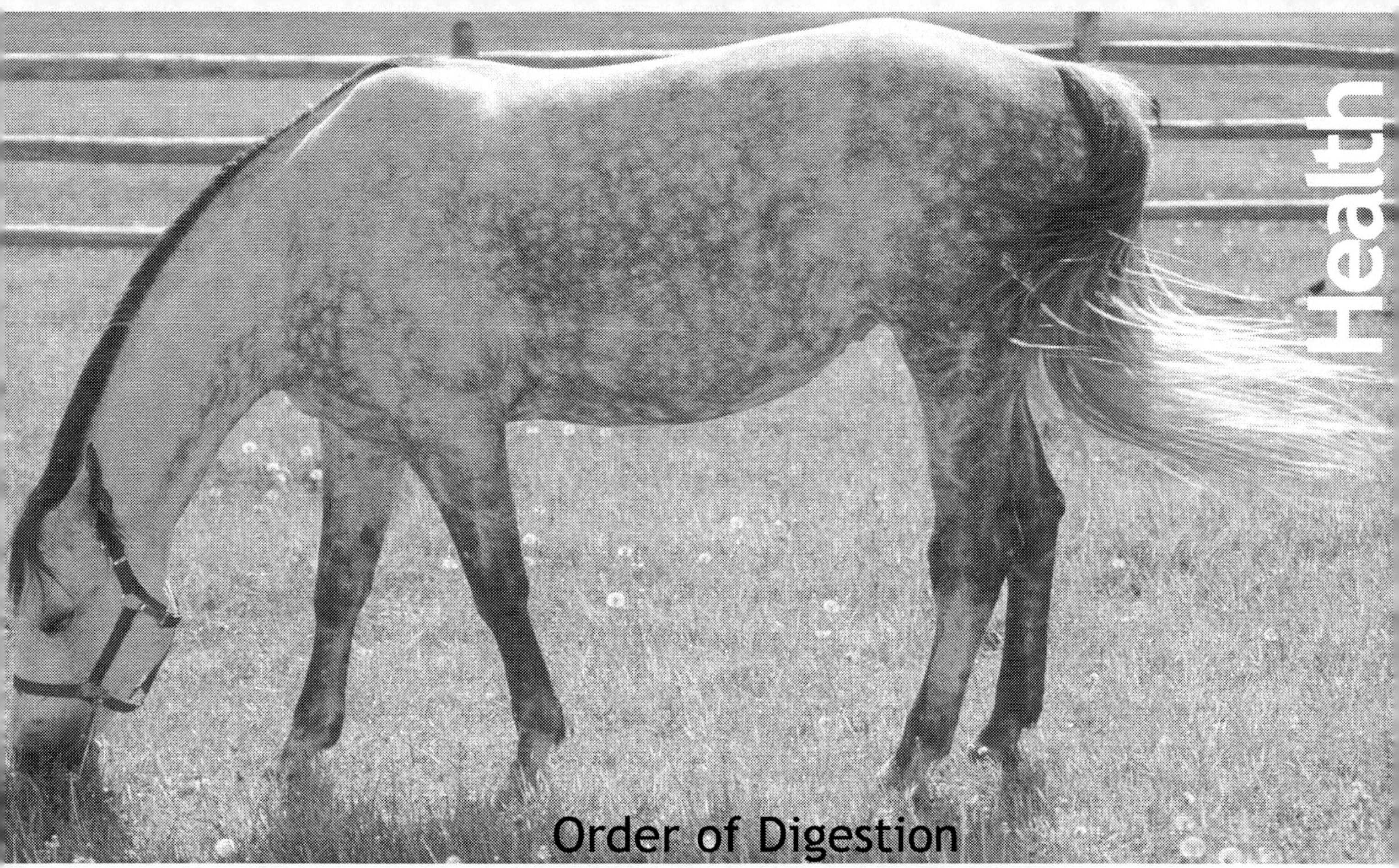

Order of Digestion

The first step in digestion is called prehension. This is the act of grasping and tearing the grass with the front teeth. The second step is mastication, which is the act of chewing the food. The third step is swallowing. Food travels down the esophagus (1) to the stomach (2). From the stomach the partially-digested food travels to the small intestine (3) and then to the caecum (4). From the caecum it passes through the large colon (5) and then the small colon (6). Undigested waste is eliminated from the rectum (7).

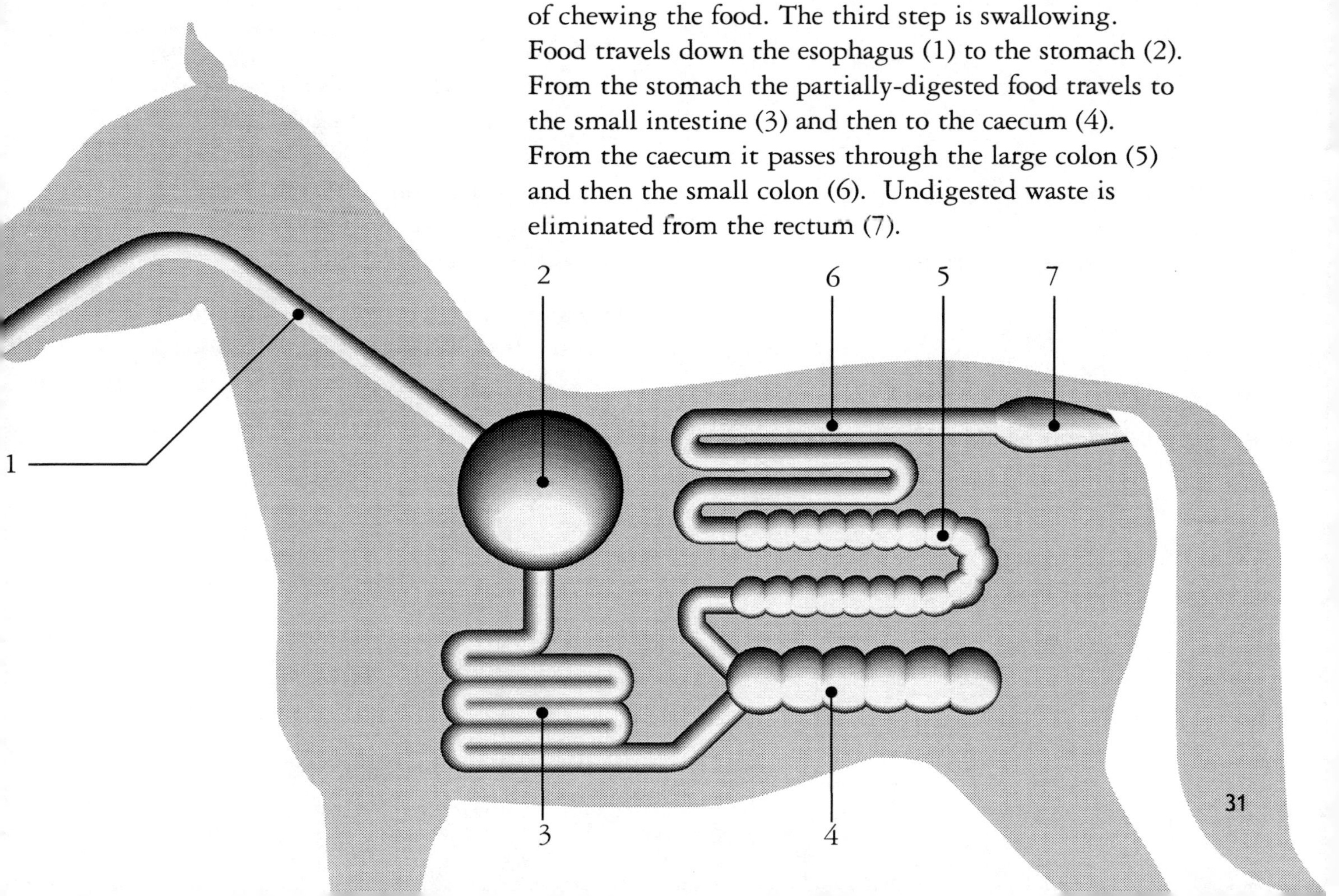

Time is the most critical factor in successfully treating colic. Some cases of colic resolve themselves without medical intervention. Many others require prompt medical care, including emergency surgery.

If you suspect a horse is suffering from colic, here is a veterinarian-recommended action plan:

1. Remove all food and water.
2. Notify your veterinarian immediately.
3. Be prepared to give your vet the following information:
   a. pulse rate (greater than 44?)
   b. respiratory rate (flared nostrils?)
   c. rectal temperature (100°F?)
   d. color of mucous membranes inside mouth (pink? moist?)
   e. Capillary Refill Time (CRT), tested by pressing gums near teeth, releasing, then counting the seconds it takes for the color to return (1 second, or more?)
   f. behavioral signs: kicking, pawing, rolling, etc.
   g. digestive noises (or lack of them?)
   h. bowel movements (color, consistency, frequency)
   i. any recent changes in management, feeding or exercise
   j. medical history, any previous episodes of abdominal pain
   k. breeding history for mares and stallions
   l. insurance status of the horse
4. Keep the horse as calm and comfortable as possible. Allow the horse to lie down if it appears quiet and resting.
5. If the horse attempts to roll or behave violently, attempt to walk the horse slowly.
6. Do not administer any medication unless specifically directed to do so by your veterinarian.
7. Follow your veterinarian's advice exactly and wait for his or her arrival.

Your veterinarian will examine your horse to determine the severity and cause of the colic. The exact steps will depend upon his or her findings. Most colics fall into one of three groups:

1. **Intestinal Dysfunction.** The most common type of colic. The horse's bowels are not working properly. It can be caused by gas pain (distension), impaction (blockage) or bowel spasms.
2. **Intestinal Accidents.** Although they occur less frequently, this type of colic includes problems like a displacement or hernia, when a section of the intestine gets trapped or pinched in the body cavity. This type of colic nearly always requires emergency surgery.
3. **Enteritis or Ulceration.** This colic is a result of inflammation, infections or lesions (cuts) within the digestive tract. It can be caused by stress, disease or parasites.

Not every case of colic is preventable, but good horse management is the best bet in reducing the risk of colic:

- Establish a daily routine of feeding, exercise and turnout
- Establish a regular de-worming routine
- Divide grain and other rations into two or more feedings per day
- Avoid feeding excessive grain/energy supplements (1/2 of your horse's energy should come from roughage (good quality hay)
- Hay is best fed "free choice"
- Provide fresh, clean water at all times
- Provide a water tank heater in cold winter weather
- Make dietary or other changes gradually
- Reduce stress. Horses stressed over changes in evironment/ workload are at a greater risk for colic
- Pay special attention to horses in transport or at horse shows
- Keep an eye on foaling mares for any signs of colic
- Maintain accurate records of management, feeding and health for each horse

Across

5 The reflex of curling the upper lip. (7,8)
6 The best way to feed hay. (4,6)
8 Choose a daily ___________ for feeding, exercise and turnout to reduce the risk of colic. (7)
10 Signs of colic vary, which is why you need to know what is __________ for your horse. (6)

Down

1 Changes in environment or routine can cause __________, creating a greater risk for colic. (6)
2 Good horse __________________ is the best way to reduce the risk of colic. (10)
3 Colic is the number one cause of __________ in horses. (5)
4 The name of the physical symptom of abdominal pain in horses. (5)
7 A term that describes an intestinal blockage. (9)
9 This is the most critical factor in successfully treating colic. (4)

Therapeutic Riding

A special bond forms between a horse and rider. Horses and humans have been together since the dawn of time. Horses have served as food, transportation, beasts of burden, in war, agriculture and sport. Today, children, youth and adults with physical and/or mental disabilities ride horses as therapy. For these special equestrians, riding a horse is both challenging and rewarding.

Magic happens when people and horses get together. Disabled riders receive physical, emotional and mental benefits. A horse moves in a gentle, repetitive rhythm similar to a person walking. The horse's rhythm and gait helps riders with physical problems improve their flexibility, balance and muscle strength. This special treatment is called hippotherapy, which comes from the Greek word ***hippos***, meaning horse. For many disabled riders, horseback riding is an opportunity to move around independently, without a wheelchair, leg braces or crutches.

For riders with mental or emotional disabilities, the special relationship with a horse provides self-confidence, patience and self-esteem. This, however, is no big secret for those who know and love horses! Maybe it's a horse's eyes? Horses have the largest eyes of any land mammal. It's easy to get lost looking into a horse's gentle and soulful eyes.

How can I get involved?

There are more than 500 therapeutic riding centers in North America. Without thousands of volunteers, therapeutic riding programs could not exist. In 1998, more than 20,000 youth and adults volunteered at programs around the country. Would you like to get involved?

Volunteers are needed to help with:

- **Leading a horse**
- **Sidewalking (walking alongside to offer rider support when needed)**
- **Grooming horses**
- **Tacking up horses**
- **Cooling out horses**
- **Cleaning tack**
- **Helping with fundraisers**

Most centers work with volunteers who are 14 years of age and older. When you volunteer your time, you learn about challenges faced by others, while learning more about horses and making new friends.

Many therapy horses are donated, volunteered or leased by horse owners in the community. More important than the breed are considerations like the horse's conformation, health, age, gaits, attitude and reliability of the horse. A variety of horses is needed to help riders with a wide range of disabilities.

You may also consider hippotherapy as a career. The American Hippotherapy Association was formed in 1993. Its members are registered physical and occupational therapists who have additional training in hippotherapy.

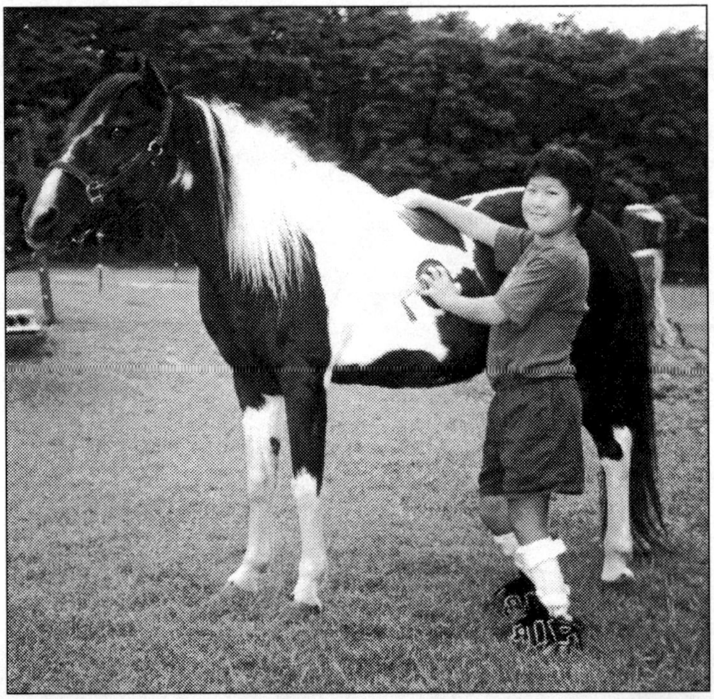

Eleven-year-old Annie Wood gets ready to compete in Western Equitation at the VanBuren County Youth Fair. Annie has spina bifida and needs both leg braces and crutches to walk. A fifth-grader at St. Mary's Elementary School in Paw Paw, Michigan, Annie is believed to be the first handicapped rider to ever compete in 4-H horse events at this fair. "Riding a horse is fun," shares Annie with a big grin. "It's only hard if you think it's hard."

For more information about therapeutic riding or to find a center near you, contact:

North American Riding For the Handicapped
PO Box 33150
Denver, CO 80233
(800) 369-7433
or visit their web site at: http://www.narha.org

Across

5 The minimum age most therapeutic riding centers accept volunteers. (8)

6 The Greek word meaning "horse." (6)

8 Riders with this kind of disability often feel more self-confident when riding a horse. (6)

10 A horse allows a person using a wheelchair to move around this way. (13)

11 The horse has the largest of these than any land mammal. (4)

12 This kind of disability makes it hard to control your feelings. (9)

Down

1 Horses served as our primary source of this until cars were invented. (14)

2 A special kind of treatment on horseback. (12)

3 Another word for "farming." (11)

4 Without these important people, therapeutic riding centers could not operate. (10)

7 Feeling good about yourself. (10)

9 This kind of disability makes it hard to walk or move around. (8)

Horse Logging

Some things never change. Draft horses continue to be used for logging. Percherons, Belgians and other big breeds provide the horsepower to help maintain forests. If you want to know about logging with horses, just ask Jason Rutledge.

"Come up, girls!" calls Rutledge. He snaps the long leather reins. With a powerful jump, Campell's Babe and Ladybug snort and lean heavily into their harness. Together these two sturdy Suffolk draft horses weigh nearly 3,200 pounds. Rutledge uses this "natural" horsepower to haul a 12-foot-long red oak log out of a Blue Ridge Mountain forest in Virginia.

As a piece of living history, Rutledge continues the trade he learned from his grandfather, a Virginia sharecropper. But horse logging is more than just an echo of the past. Clear-cutting of trees by big machines like trucks and bulldozers is a concern for many landowners today. "Horse loggers imitate nature, selectively harvesting through a process of single tree selection," explains fellow logger Jagger Rutledge, Jason's 18 year old son. "We walk the forest, looking for damaged/ diseased and mature trees. By removing these trees, we help keep a natural balance in the forest."

Selectively harvesting trees has a minimum impact on the habitat and wildlife. The only traces a horse logger leaves behind are hoof prints and the narrow skid mark from the dragging log. The Rutledge crew carefully fell a chosen tree, directing where it will fall. They keep both safety and forest impact in mind as they bring down the tree with chain saws. But that is only the beginning.

Once a tree is "felled," the loggers "limb" the tree to remove all the branches. The tree is then measured and "bucked" into eight, ten or twelve-foot lengths. Tree species and quality determine the log lengths. In Appalachia, the Rutledge crew commonly harvests red and white oak, white pine and tulip poplar trees. While all of this is happening, other workers are busy clearing a "skid trail" to get the log out of the forest and to the waiting truck.

Once a log is ready to go, the team of horses is hitched to the "log arch." This is a special buggy designed especially for logging. The log is attached to the log arch with a thick heavy chain wrapped around one end. Next, the team of horses is backed up and hitched to the front of the log arch. The driver takes up contact with the reins, releases the lines and calls "Come up!" This is the signal to pull.

In an average day, the Rutledge teams pull around 25 logs out of the forest. A single log can weigh 3,000 pounds, only 200 pounds less than the team of horses themselves! Jason Rutledge is proud of the inheritance he has passed on to his son, who also plans a career in logging. "Conventional logging is sort of "fast-food" forestry," he explains. "This is what I call real "home-cooking!"

Down

1 This attaches the log to the log arch. (5)
2 A mountainous region of the United States. (10)
3 This type of selection helps horse loggers imitate nature. (6,4)
4 The command used to tell the horse team to pull together. (4,2)
6 A unique breed of draft horse, suited for heavy pulling. (7)
7 This form of mechanized tree harvesting takes down every tree in the forest. (5,7)
8 This has to be cleared so the team can drag the log out of the forest. (4,5)
9 The logger's word for cutting down a tree. (7)
10 A logger's term for cutting a tree into lengths of log. (7)

Across

5 Only these and a skid trail are left behind from horse logging. (4,6)
8 The occupation of Mr. Rutledge's grandfather. (12)
11 The horses are hitched to this to pull a log. (3,4)
12 The process of removing all the branches from a tree after it is cut. (7)
13 The state where you will find the Blue Ridge Mountains. (8)

the colder regions of North
nerica, loggers often choose to cut
d haul trees during winter. With
ow on the ground, horse-drawn
ds can also be used to haul wood.

Endurance Riding

Do you enjoy spending time in the saddle? How would you like to join a group of horses and riders who cover a minimum of fifty miles per day? The endurance riding motto is: "To finish is to win."

For the most serious riders, the endurance race is a highly competitive and challenging athletic event. For others it is more like combining a camping trip with a very long trail ride. People of all ages enjoy the challenge of endurance riding. (For us beginners there are limited distance rides that are ONLY twenty-five miles long!)

Participants who successfully complete the Western States 100 Miles-One Day Ride are rewarded with a commemorative silver buckle. The buckle was inspired by the famous historical painting by Herman Hansen entitled "Indian Gauntlet," depicting the speed and courage of the Pony Express Rider.

There is much more to endurance riding than completing the course in the fastest time. The focus of an endurance event is to finish the race on a sound and healthy horse. Although endurance rides are technically 'races,' many horse and rider teams participate for completion rather than winning. To these riders the satisfaction of completing a fifty mile event is the prize. In an endurance race, every horse and rider team that finishes "sound and healthy" receives an award, which they have surely earned.

U.S. Cavalry soldiers were the models for endurance riders today. These military horse and rider teams were conditioned over long distances and rough terrain. The key to success in endurance riding is a blend of teamwork and proper conditioning. This unique sport values fitness above all. Riders have to be in great shape as well. Serious endurance riders will often dismount and jog beside their horses for several miles.

In an endurance race, the horse and rider team with the fastest time is the winner, as long as the horse passes the 'fit to continue' checkup from the veterinarian. Throughout the ride veterinarians monitor every horse in the race at predetermined checkpoints. Any horse judged to be unsound or physically unfit must withdraw from the competition. At each vet check, the horse's soundness, heart rate and hydration are evaluated. Each endurance race also has mandatory rests or 'holds' for the horses throughout the ride.

The American Endurance Ride Conference (AERC) was founded in 1972 as a national governing and record keeping body for long distance horse riding. Over the years, it has developed rules and guidelines to give endurance events a standard format and strict veterinary controls. Basic rules require that endurance rides be at least 50 miles in length per day (some rides are 100-mile per day events!). Any breed or type of horse or mule is eligible, provided it is at least 5 years of age.

JOKE

Where does a horse go when it loses its tail?

Trilby Pederson of San José, California aboard her most famous endurance riding partner, Rushcreek Lad. Together Trilby and her magnificent Arabian Hall of Fame Horse completed more than 20,000 endurance-riding miles. In 1987 alone they completed more than 4,000 miles. Trilby began endurance riding in 1982 at the age of 48. Still riding today at age 65, Trilby has ridden more than 45,000 endurance miles and is making application to the Guinness Book of World Records.

Would you like to try endurance riding? Is there a fifty-mile event in your future?

To learn more about endurance riding, write to:

The American Endurance Ride Conference
11960 Heritage Oak Place, Suite 9
Auburn, CA 95603

or check out their web site at www.AERC.com In addition to promoting the sport of endurance riding, the AERC also supports the use, protection and development of equestrian trails across the U.S.

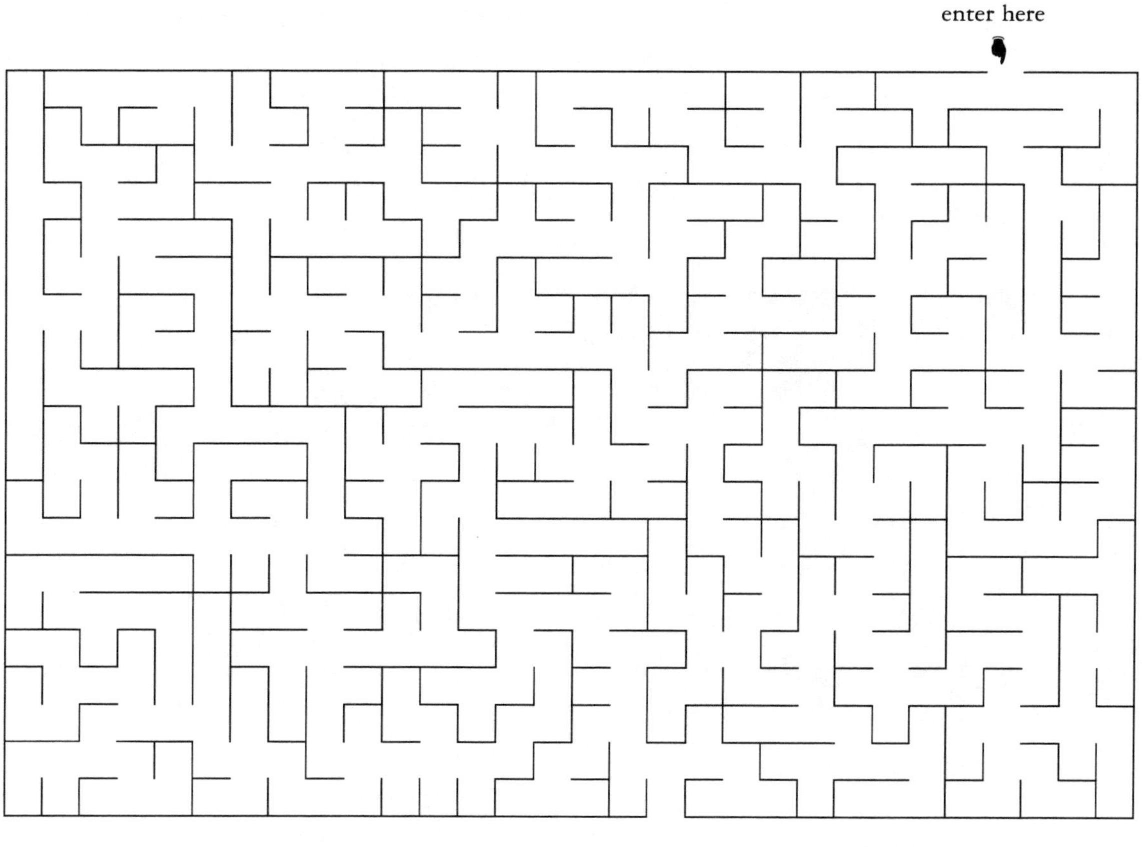

Spotlight on Dressage

Have you ever danced with your horse? The term "dressage" comes to us from a French word that means "training" (it rhymes with the word "massage"). The basics of classical horsemanship were first written down by Xenephon, a Greek general who lived around 400 B.C. Over the centuries, this form of riding was developed by the royal courts of Europe. The famous white Lipizzan stallions of the Spanish Riding School in Vienna, Austria, along with their riders, dedicate their lives to the performance of classical riding.

Today dressage is both a riding discipline and a competitive sport open to all horses and riders. The goal of dressage training is to develop the horse's three natural gaits, balance, tempo, suppleness and obedience. Any horse and rider team can improve by learning some of the basic dressage exercises and movements. It also improves the seat, coordination and "feel" of the rider, as the rider learns to communicate with subtle cues. These cues can be nearly invisible, such as a simple shift of weight in the saddle or light leg pressure.

There are three basic dressage exercises. The first are figures, such as serpentines and circles. The second are movements, such as lateral (sideways) movements. The third are transitions, such as trot-to-halt or walk-to-canter. These are all wonderful exercises for starting a young horse or re-training an older horse. As the horse and rider progress, more difficult exercises are added. Together a horse and rider learn to work in harmony while performing with grace and athletic ability.

Dressage is a world-wide competitive sport. It first became an Olympic sport in 1912. The United States proudly brought home the Bronze medal from the 1992 Olympic Games in Barcelona, Spain. Although only a very few horses have the physical ability and temperament to succeed at the Olympic level, dressage riders can set their own goals and successfully compete at lower levels of this beautiful equine sport.

Local schooling shows are a great chance for dressage beginners. You should visit a dressage show to learn more about the sport. The first thing you will notice is that all dressage competitions take place in a rectangular arena of exact measurements. A standard size dressage arena is 20 x 60 meters (66 feet x 197 feet). Large letters are placed at specific points along the outer rail. They serve as markers or targets for performing figures, movements and transitions.

Here I am aboard my 7 year-old Thoroughbred/Percheron mare, Sonata. A dressage rookie on a novice dressage horse, Sonata carried me back in the show ring for the first time in nearly 24 years! We competed at several schooling shows this summer, riding the USDF walk/trot tests. Here we are at the beginning of a test, with me mentally reciting: "A" enter working trot, "C" track left. One of the best things about dressage is how much it is like bowling. Even if you mess up on one movement, you can always ride a "strike" on the next one. (We scored a "7" for the movement in the photo!)

If you have watched or competed in English or Western pleasure classes, you may be surprised. Dressage competitors perform their "tests" in the arena one at a time. Both horse and rider team are judged and scored individually. At the sound

One of the Tempel Lipizzan stallions performing the Levade. The horse rises on his haunches from a standstill position and tucks his forelegs under him as he maintains a 45 degree angle The Levade is often the pose of classical equestrian sculpture and art. Located in Wadsworth, IL, the Tempel Farms Lipizzanners perform shows for the public twice weekly. For more info. call (847) 623-7272.

of the judge's bell or whistle, the rider has one minute to enter the arena and begin the designated test. Most tests begin with the horse and rider entering the arena at the "A" marker, halting in the center at the "C" marker and saluting the judge. (At the Introductory and Training Levels, most tests consist of simple obedience at a brisk walk, trot and canter along the rail or in large circles or serpentines.)

The judge observes the horse and rider, evaluating each "movement" against a standard of perfection which ranges from 0 (meaning not executed) to 10 (meaning excellent). Some difficult movements have their scores multiplied by two. The judge makes her comments and gives each score aloud to a "scribe," who makes quick notes on the scoresheet for the rider to read later. The judge looks for correct execution of movements and figures, as well as the quality of the horse's impulsion (forward energy), and submission (relaxation and obedience). There is also a score given for the rider's position, balance, harmony and effectiveness.

To learn more about dressage, write the
United States Dressage Federation
PO Box 6669
Lincoln, NE 68506-0669
or visit them online at www.usdf.org.

Across

4 A difficult dressage movement with the horse rising on his haunches and tucking his forelegs under himself. (6)

7 The U.S. Olympic Dressage Team brought this medal home from Spain in 1992. (6)

8 Dressage is French for this word. (8)

9 A type of local dressage show for novice and intermediate dressage riders. (9)

11 These famous white stallions perform difficult classical movements. (8)

12 Another word for forward energy. (9)

13 These kinds of dressage exercises can include a sideways movement. (9)

Down

1 These types of dressage exercises involving changing from one gait to another. (11)

2 This famous Greek horseman lived in 400 B.C. (8)

3 The shape of a standard dressage arena. (9)

5 The country that is home to the Spanish Riding School of Vienna. (7)

6 These dressage exercises include circles and serpentines. (7)

9 This person assists a dressage judge by writing down scores and comments. (6)

10 After entering the dressage ring, the rider halts and does this. (6)

The First Saturday in May

On the first Saturday in May, thousands of spectators gather every year to watch the Kentucky Derby in Louisville, KY. The annual "Run for the Roses" is the oldest continuously running sporting event in U.S. history. The first Derby ran in 1875, making the 1999 Derby the 125th Kentucky Derby.

The Kentucky Derby is a mile-and-a-quarter race held every year at Churchill Downs Park. The fastest three-year old Thoroughbred colts and fillies and their jockeys thunder around the track, trying to win a place in history in less than two minutes.

Since 1952, the Kentucky Derby is a nationally televised media event, watched by millions around the world. Even people who take no interest in horses during the rest of the year are interested in the names and stories of the horses favored to win this year's Derby. The city of Louisville celebrates for two weeks before the Derby. On the day of the race, nearly 150,000 spectators fill the grandstand and infield to get a glimpse of the race.

African Americans played an important role in U.S. Thoroughbred racing history, serving as grooms, trainers and jockeys. The great African American jockey Oliver Lewis aboard Aristides won the first Kentucky Derby. Of the 14 horses running in the Derby that first year (1875), 12 of them were ridden by black jockeys, most of them were sons of former slaves.

Tidbits

- Only three fillies have even won the Kentucky Derby:
  - Regret (1915)
  - Genuine Risk (1980)
  - Winning Colors (1988)
- Diane Crump aboard Fathom was the first female jockey to win the Kentucky Derby in 1970.
- Determine (1954) was the first gray Thoroughbred to win the Kentucky Derby. He also sired the 1962 Derby winner, Decidedly.
- Of the seven basic Thoroughbred colors (black, brown/bay, dark bay, red/chestnut, gray, roan, white), a white-colored Thoroughbred is the only color that has not won the Derb
- Jockeys Eddie Acaro and Bill Hartack are tied for the record of Derby wins, with 5 each.
- Pre-Derby favorites do not necessarily win. The last "favorite" to win the Derby was Spectacular Bid in 1979.
- Calumet Farms in Kentucky have bred an incredible eight Kentucky Derby winners.
- The traditional song played before each Kentucky Derby is "My Old Kentucky Home."
- Since 1973 Secretariat has held the current record for the Derby at 1 minute, 59²/5ths seconds.

Secretariat

Kentucky Derby Winners 1875-1936

G M M S Y S P C T I D U A L P V E C O R Q J V D B D Z B R O
Q W F R P H V K L R M U S R A O J K P S L N M D C Y A C U X
G K M W A O R Q U U S M P O U K F P P Q E G Q F Y W T X Y D
E L G W Y M K C X I F U E D L F N Y S J L M Q J V S U T B Z
O U K N N A N A H C U B J D J X X U Z I E Q J G I I O O O W
O N X O O R G N N Q A O J U O F D X L K U E C A D K Q Z I G
B E S S B K S X G E N X L U N R J X O Q N D E T P N X S J S
A V S B E H A V E Y O U R S E L F C S K A J O I I C V H C F
A U T I G A O Z O U D P A G S I W J C M M S I R S M V U P R
F R O G N Y H P R U M D R O L I T H X J G E K C T G S Y H X
S J N T I Y Z U G A A E L J E H R V I L N M U M I R A O M K
E U E N Y A N W E Y T U W B R E Z B X S I R H U O N D G M E
U X S A L M A H S E M I H E G D U J A Q K A S N C R W F E U
L B T N F R Q R M Q L A I Y P R F R P R B E U R A O V M Q E
Y Y R E V O G N I L B B U B G J D A Y S T A R Y N C M I F C
L V E T R U N O T T O C E O J O I T Y G I O B Y U A Y A C K
M N E U I M H S H T B Z O L D R O S E B U D N F I V V P H H
O M T E L R I C O W J K E D A K G K E X M G E W E A W O I A
R G G I E C S N H E I K Z V A A I N W B A Y B O G L Y L N O
P L C L Y D E V A N D U S E N O A I C L C Y U R G C W L D H
H H E M U T M G G T L Y C N Z L N P L A B E A T O A K O O L
G S X E X T I S E Y O P N T I T N A H C E N Y H R D N O O I
N A O R C K N D Y G E R D U E D N J A K T P B I A E T K A D
N Z C I S S E D B R O K E R S T I P A G H E S O R T N O M Z
H N E D A B N E D A B S G E F O O K V O I T D A V A L U A C
X R E I G H C O U N T R Q O H E G H O L I L I C H P F T R W
R X G A D I E L E D E N X A A L A N A D A L E O N A T U S O
B E N N L R A F I E J H H A U X I X E T H Z Y L K X L T I Z
F Y B Q I W Y K N O E N F C I I I S W R I E L Q S T W M E A
R U S R D V Q L B Z V U R G H S C Q Q B J F K I A N D A A D

Agile (1905)
Alanadale (1902)
Apollo (1882)
Aristides (1875)
Azra (1892)
Baden Baden (1877)
Behave Yourself (1921)
Ben Ali (1886)
Ben Brush (1896)
Black Gold (1924)
Bold Venture (1936)
Brokers Tip (1933)
Bubbling Over (1926)
Buchanan (1884)
Burgoo King (1932)
Cavalcade (1934)
Chant (1894)
Clyde Van Dusen (1929)
Day Star (1878)
Donau (1910)
Donerail (1913)
Elwood (1904)
Exterminator (1918)
Flying Ebony (1925)
Fonso (1880)
Gallant Fox (1930)
George Smith (1916)
Halma (1895)
Hindoo (1881)
His Eminence (1901)
Joe Cotton (1885)
Judge Himes (1903)
Kingman (1891)
Leonatus (1883)
Lieutenant Gibson (1900)
Lookout (1893)
Lord Murphy (1879)
Macbeth II (1888)
Manuel (1899)
Meridian (1911)
Montrose (1887)
Morvich (1922)
Old Rosebud (1914)
Omaha (1935)
Omar Khayyam (1917)
Paul Jones (1920)
Pink Star (1907)
Plaudit (1898)
Regret (1915)
Reigh Count (1928)
Riley (1890)
Sir Barton (1919)
Sir Huon (1906)
Spokane (1889)
Stone Street (1908)
Twenty Grand (1931)
Typhoon II (1897)
Vagrant (1876)
Whiskery (1927)
Wintergreen (1909)
Worth (1912)
Zev (1923)

Sir Barton

Kentucky Derby Winners 1937-1995

W I W N K K J B K Z R V K D N L Z C B A H X Z B N P A R J U
I J K K O M M M W Y O L A H S ' Y N N U S O A H D X P S C G
B R A C C C R E A L Q U I E T P P K V Y U Q U Z S E V N T J
Y S O R E H A E S J S R H C L U G R E D N U H T M A Y Z I F
L O G N H U H R E Y E W Z G X H Y Q M I D D L E G R O U N D
D A Q J L G C D S N B S A A L Y S H E B A W W K G I L P U G
E Y E G D I R A V I R T T P Q U C A R R Y B A C K A J D N J
D R U D H C E N D F O O L I S H P L E A S U R E D N O P B C
I A P N K O V G S D F Z B S C T J G C L I C T H O O P J R .
C O U N T F L E E T D C G H U P X B N U L M W X Q B A E I V
E E T . E L I L A N L P Z Y W S R Q A C E N I M R E T E D X
D X U H E P S W T U O T U H S Y L I D A N F T T J D P L L L
O E S W L O W P T W B G P L E A S A N T C O L O N Y G H E A
Z G G X L I A G L L I H F R V W W N R C E R A T S K R A D E
Z A T A I R A T E R C E S E M W H O E E E W S L Y C M C B N
B I Y Z L I C S S D J R N I Y Z T I H P K A F W W U Y F U X
W Z N Q I L K D L O G E H T E K I R T S Z R A V N L Z D P X
C A N N O N A D E N T D V A N O L A R I M D A R A W G O R D
Y A W A L R I H W I N N I N G C O L O R S P E N D A B U C K
V K J C H A T E A U G A Y W S E A C N N Y A N Y U L W O D U
J I W B U G J N Y D Z M Z U S W N D L E Z S V P J H U I K X
K D L M T F W W D Z I M L T R H I U Z O D S W S E N T A X G
N F T F C A N O N E R O I I E P G O I Q N * R W T N U F P S
K E E L Y M O T A D P C N M R N R R V N Q F O T P A S F I K
E M E Q R I S S N O I T A T I C O P L D E B U U I K W I T Y
J H X D E Z S N I X B S U A K F F T A C Q R P K L V S R V W
P C H R L A O H D T E U O M G G O M W Y F T I A O P I M X E
Y N U V U E T O R R W D G Y J H G C G R I N D S T O N E X A
N K E L A W S J E V N C U G J M G Y A M G V L W K Q E D U K
Z U T N Q S Q U F X P Y Q H J H Y R H Y N B R N R O V J R B

One of the most famc
Thoroughbreds of thi
tury was Man O'War.
However, he did not
the Triple Crown as a
3 year-old in 1920
because he was not
entered in the Kentu
Derby. He ran away v
both the Preakness ar
the Belmont Stakes.

Affirmed (1978)
Alysheba (1987)
Assault (1946)
Bold Forbes (1976)
Cannonade (1974)
Canonero II (1971)
Carry Back (1961)
Chateaugay (1963)
Citation (1948)
Count Fleet (1943)
Count Turf (1951)
Dark Star (1953)
Decidedly (1962)
Determine (1954)
Dust Commander (1970)
Ferdinand (1986)
Foolish Pleasure (1975)
Forward Pass (1968) *
Gallahadion (1940)
Gato del Sol (1982)
Genuine Risk (1980)
Go for Gin (1994)
Grindstone (1996)
Hill Gail (1952)
Hoop Jr. (1945)
Iron Liege (1957)
Jet Pilot (1947)
Johnstown (1939)
Kauai King (1966)
Lawrin (1938)
Lil E. Tee (1992)
Lucky Debonair (1965)
Majestic Prince (1969)
Middleground (1950)
Needles (1956)
Northern Dancer (1964)
Pensive (1944)
Pleasant Colony (1981)
Ponder (1949)
Proud Clarion (1967)
Real Quiet (1998)
Riva Ridge (1972)
Sea Hero (1993)
Seattle Slew (1977)
Secretariat (1973)
Shut Out (1942)
Silver Charm (1997)
Spectacular Bid (1979)
Spend a Buck (1985)
Strike the Gold (1991)
Sunday Silence (1989)
Sunny's Halo (1983)
Swale (1984)
Swaps (1955)
Thunder Gulch (1995)
Tim Tam (1958)
Tomy Lee (1959)
Unbridled (1990)
Venetian Way (1960)
War Admiral (1937)
Whirlaway (1941)
Winning Colors (1988)

A total of 43
Thoroughbre
have finished
win shy of th
Triple Crown

Gallant Fox i
only Triple C
winner to eve
another Tripl
Crown winne
Omaha.

* Dancer's Image finished first in the 1968 Derby, but was disqualified when a post-race exam revealed traces of a drug that was banned in racing at that time. That same drug is now accepted, but the disqualification stands.

Triple Crown Winners

						A	R						
						M	C						
						V	O						
		M	R	E		L	D		N	T	D		
	J	Z	V	B	A	X	T	C	Q	H	Q	C	
R	H	Q	F	L	N	O	T	R	A	B	R	I	S
T	N	R	S	T	T	F	D	X	W	H	N	T	E
A	A	N	E	R	L	T	O	R	E	D	K	A	C
H	W	S	C	O	U	N	T	F	L	E	E	T	I
Z	F	R	R	O	A	A	W	Y	S	M	U	I	T
J	D	S	E	V	S	L	A	A	E	R	R	O	S
W	L	V	T	X	S	L	R	W	L	I	K	N	S
	O	M	A	H	A	A	A	A	T	F	Z	L	
	L	S	R	Z	Y	G	D	L	T	F	M	G	
		S	I	Q	Y	X	M	R	A	A	I		
		T	A	C	R	A	I	I	E	G	C		
			T	E	H	Q	R	H	S	D			
			O	O	D	D	A	W	Q	L			
					X	D	L	C					

Affirmed (1978)
Assault (1946)
Citation (1948)
Count Fleet (1943)
Gallant Fox (1930)
Omaha (1935)
Seattle Slew (1977)
Secretariat (1973)
Sir Barton (1919)
War Admiral (1937)
Whirlaway (1941)

When Seattle Slew won the Triple Crown in 1977, followed by Affirmed in 1978, it was the only time there have ever been back-to-back Triple Crown winners.

iple Crown con-
the Kentucky
the Preakness
Belmont Stakes.

Twenty-five years went by after Citation won the Triple Crown in 1948. Some thought there might never be another Triple Crown winner until Secretariat came along in 1973.

The Triple Crown is the most difficult feat in Thoroughbred racing. Only three year-old colts have ever accomplished it. (A filly has never won the Triple Crown.)

The Amazing Fire Horse

How did fireman fight fires before they had motorized fire engines? Any breed of horse could pull a milk wagon, but it was a special horse that was chosen to pull a fire wagon. These special horses were often Percherons, Belgians, Morgans or a mixture of those breeds. These amazing horses were brave, intelligent and fast. Weighing at least 1400 pounds each, the teams of two or three horses were often matched for size and color to add to their spectacular appearance.

To become a fire horse in the 1800's, the fire department's veterinarian first checked each candidate. Then the horse was "field-tested" by pulling a carriage. If the horse passed these two steps, it was sent either to fire horse college or to on-the-job training at a fire station. Larger cities, such as Detroit, Michigan, had training schools for fire horses.

Either two or three horses were assigned to each steamer engine, depending upon the weight of the steamer and the steepness of any hills in the area. The horses' stalls were beside the engine, so that the horses could quickly back into place when an alarm sounded. The typical response time after the first alarm bell was to be hitched and out the door in only 40-60 seconds.

One of the inventions used by firemen to get the horses hitched quickly was the swinging harness. When the alarm sounded, the stall doors opened automatically and the harnesses dropped down from the ceiling onto the horses. The waiting watchman quickly finished the hitching and they would rush out the door to the fire.

Fire horses spent most of their time in their stalls, waiting for the alarm to sound. They were the well-loved pets of the fireman and the entire neighborhood. When fire horses were replaced by motorized fire engines in this century, these amazing horses were retired or sold for other uses, such as pulling a delivery wagon. There are true stories of former fire horses responding to an alarm and running behind a fire engine to a fire, pulling their milk wagon behind them. This is where the expression "like an old fire horse" came from.

Here is a fireman describing one of his horses, from an 1897 edition of *The Fireman's Herald*: "Dan is the pride of the New York Fire Department. He is probably eighteen years old, and has been attached to Company No. 4 the greater part of his life. He will "shake hands" as a greeting to visitors, and he displays wonderful masculine instinct in his preference for fair womankind when asked for a kiss. He will kiss a beautiful lady with evident relish. He has never been ill during all these years, and has run with the machine to 3,600 fires, and there has never been a fire below Houston Street to which he has not responded."

To learn more about fire horses, look for a fire museum near you. A state-by-state directory of fire museums can be found at: http://firemuseumnetwork.org/dir.html

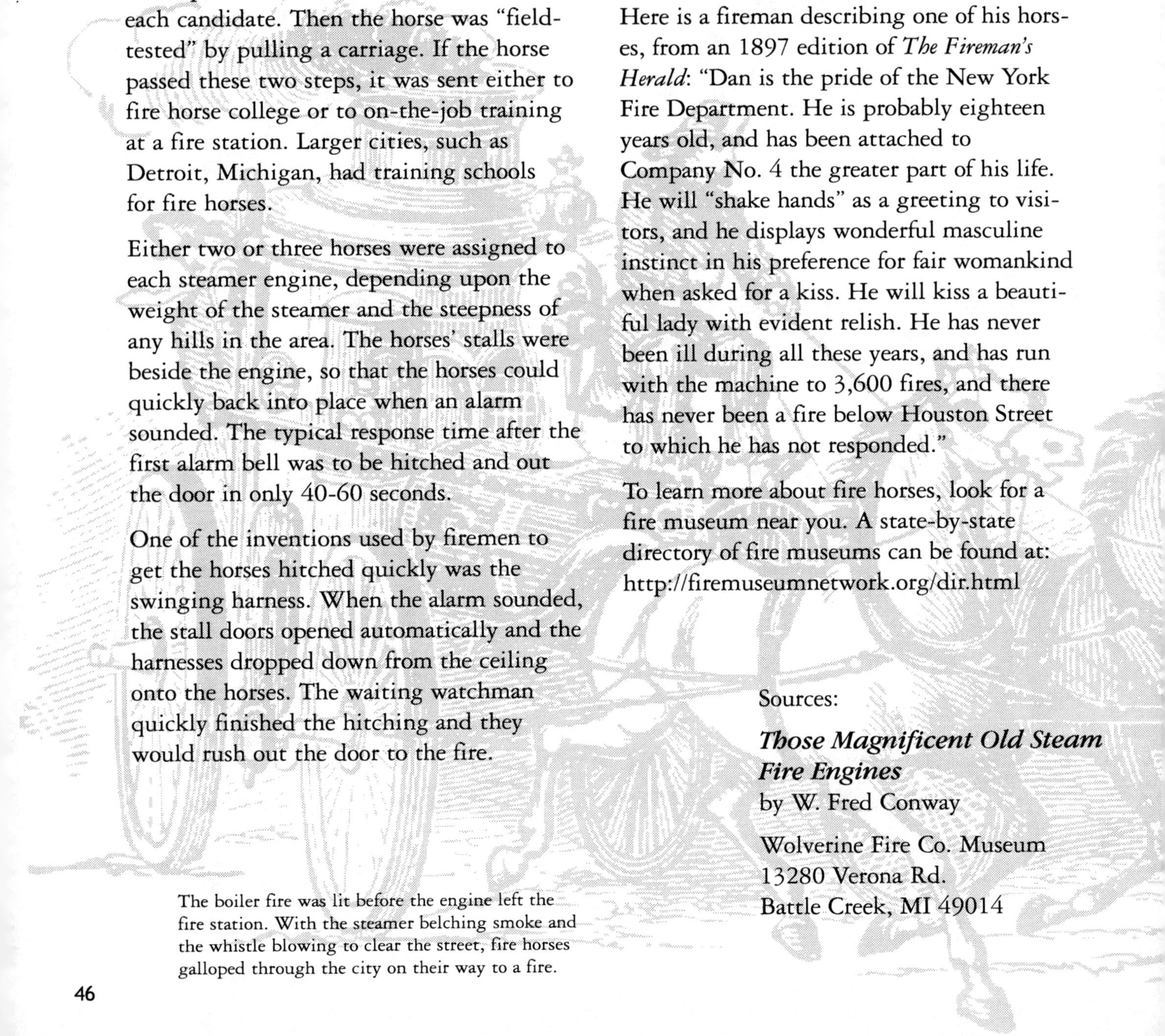

The boiler fire was lit before the engine left the fire station. With the steamer belching smoke and the whistle blowing to clear the street, fire horses galloped through the city on their way to a fire.

Sources:

Those Magnificent Old Steam Fire Engines
by W. Fred Conway

Wolverine Fire Co. Museum
13280 Verona Rd.
Battle Creek, MI 49014

Across

4 The ______ of the steamer determined whether there were 2 or 3 horses hitched. (6)

6 Because a fire was lit in the boiler, this poured out of the steamer as it raced to a fire. (5)

7 This blew to clear the streets ahead. (7)

9 This city had a special college for fire horses. (7)

11 Fire horses were often matched for ________. (4)

12 How ________ the hills were mad a difference in how many horses were in a hitch. (5)

13 Large draft breed, usually sorrel or chesnut in color. (7)

Down

1 Fire horses were also matched for _______. (5)

2 This draft breed is ususually black or grey. (9)

3 Where fire horses spent most of their lives. (5)

5 Stalls were located ___________ the steamer engine for quick hitches. (6)

8 This kind of harness dropped from the ceiling. (8)

10 This strong breed was named for the schoolmaster owner of the foundation stallion. (6)

11 This powered the fire engine's pumps. (5)

Here is a reprint from the catalog of the George C. Hale Company of Kansas City, Missouri. This early 1900's catalog company supplied the Hale Swinging Harness and other fire department supplies to cities across the United States.

The Western Reining Horse

This equestrian athlete is famous for "stopping on a dime and giving you a nickel's change." Reining is a Western performance pattern ridden accurately and at great speed. Like a dressage test, the horse and rider perform a predetermined pattern, which a judge scores.

Reining patterns require a highly trained horse and a very skilled rider. Each pattern includes quick stops and starts, rapid changes of direction, flying lead changes, pivots, spins and rollbacks. During a pivot, the horse turns 90-degrees from a halt by pivoting on his hindquarters. Both front feet completely leave the ground and do not touch it again until the pivot is complete.

A spin is a 360-degree turn on the hindquarters. A spin usually begins with the horse being reined into a sliding stop from a fast lope. After the spin is completed, the rider cues the horse to lope off on a specific lead.

The rollback is another reining movement that begins with a quick or sliding stop from the lope. The rider cues the horse to roll around on his hocks, making a 180-degree turn. A horse performing a well-executed rollback will bring his front feet down in the tracks it just made. After the rollback is complete, the horse is asked to lope straightaway on a specific lead.

RIDDLE

A cowboy rode to an inn on Friday, stayed two nights, and left on Friday. How could that be?

Beaded Bandana

A fun craft item to wear that requires no sewing!

Items needed:
one bandana
pony beads (available at craft stores)
iron
scissors
ruler
chalk

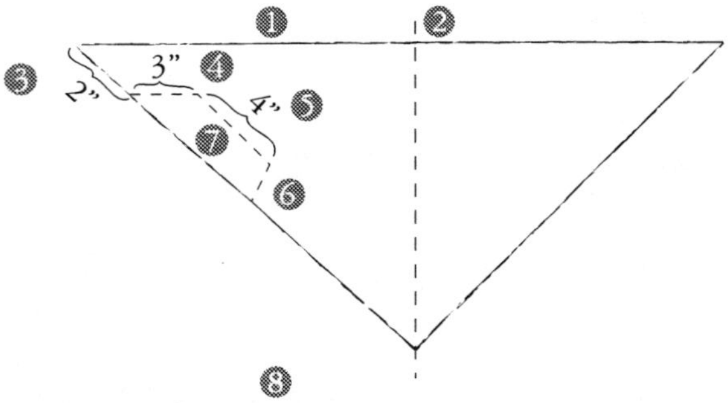

1. Fold the bandana in half so it looks like a triangle.
2. Press along the fold with a warm iron. (Get help from an adult if you need it.)

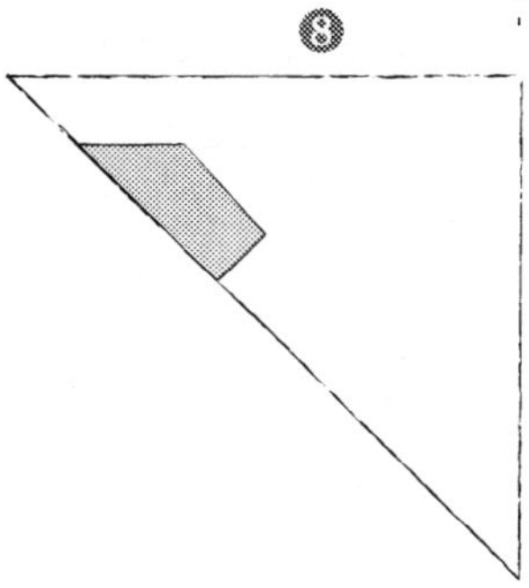

3. Use a ruler to measure down one side of the triangle 2 inches. Mark the spot with your chalk.
4. Measure across 3 inches and draw this line with your chalk.
5. Measure down the bandana 4 inches and draw this line with your chalk.
6. Draw your last line straight down to the edge of the triangle.

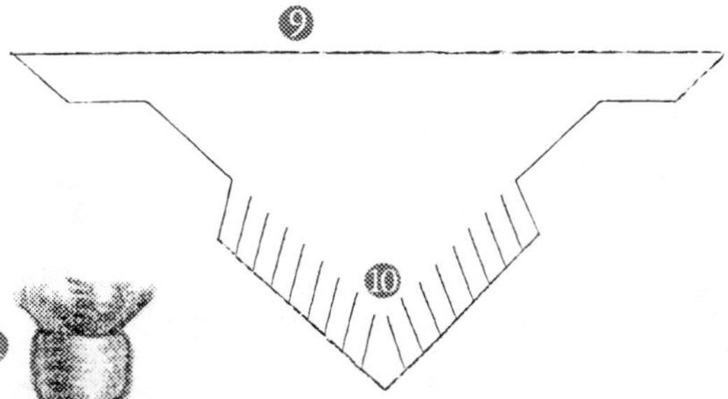

7. Use your scissors to cut out the shape you have just drawn.
8. Fold the bandana in half and cut out the same shape on the other side.

11

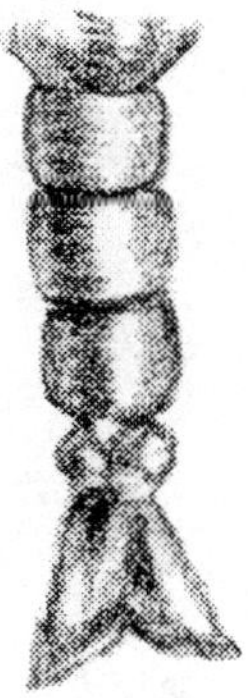

9. Open the bandana up again so it looks like a triangle.
10. Start from the bottom point and use your scissors to cut slashes up both sides of the bandana, cutting a 3 inch slash every half inch or so.
11. Thread 4-5 pony beads onto each slash and tie the end with a square knot.
12. Wear the bandana tied in front or in back!

12

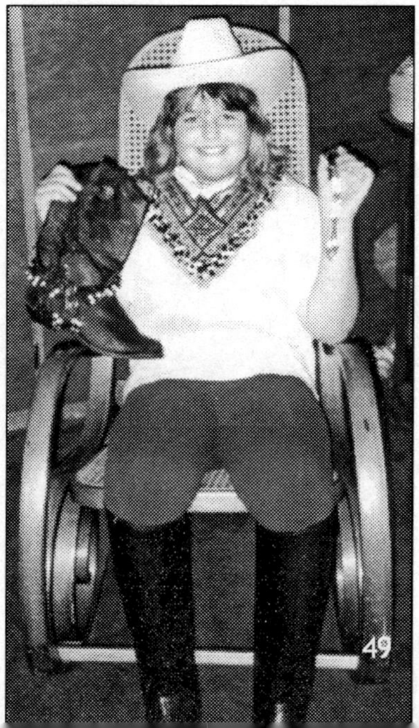

"In the winter I made beaded bandanas, boot bracelets, hat bands, and key chains to sell. I sold them at 4H tack sales. I earned $145. I bought my helmet (ASTM), english boots, stock pin, english saddle pad, and a barrette." Liz Wood, age 10.

Stuffed Molasses Apples

Terrific for a special treat or hiding medication.

Ingredients:

- 2 large apples
- 1 cup bran
- 1 carrot, shredded
- 1/3 cup molasses
- 1/2 cup brown sugar
- 1/2 cup sweet feed
- 2 sprigs of parsley or green carrot top
- confectioner's sugar

Core two apples and dig out as much of the center as you can, as you would a pumpkin at Halloween. Set this aside.

Mix shredded carrot with bran, molasses, brown sugar and sweet feed in a large bowl. Add more molasses or bran to give the mixture a stiff consistency. Scoop mixture out of the bowl and press into cored apples. Press fairly tightly.

To garnish: Drip a small amount of molasses over the top so it runs down the sides of the apple. Add a sprig of parsley or carrot greens, top with a seedless green grape, sprinkle with confectioner's sugar and serve IMMEDIATELY! Serve in a feed bucket as this is a gooey treat. Serves two horses.

Applesauce Bute Lumps

Ingredients:

- 1/2 cup applesauce
- 1 to 2 cups oatmeal
- 3 to 4 tablespoons sugar
- 1 tablespoon molasses

Mix ingredients together and add enough oatmeal to form a thick paste. Keeps about 10 days in the refrigerator. When you are ready to medicate your horse, scoop out a spoonful, big enough to bury the bute pill. You can break the pill in half or you can bury the whole pill within the lump.

For added garnish: Coat the lump by dropping in a baggie filled with oatmeal. To keep your hands clean, insert the pill after placing the lump in the bag. Squeeze pill into lump through plastic.

Since bute pills are bitter and dissolve quickly, don't add them until you are ready to medicate — usually right outside the stall.

A final suggestion: Feed your horse one lump without the bute pill, a second with the pill, and a third without. He'll assume he's receiving nothing but treats!

Mom's Apple Spice Muffins

Ingredients:

- 1 cup flour
- 1 cup wheat germ
- 1/2 teaspoon cinnamon
- 1/2 cup sugar
- 1/2 teaspoon salt
- 1 tablespoon baking powder
- 1 egg
- 2/3 cup milk
- 1/4 cup corn oil
- 1 cup apples, chopped (Macintosh preferred)

Preheat oven to 400°. Generously grease muffin tins.

In a large bowl, mix dry ingredients together and set aside. In a separate bowl, mix thoroughly the remaining ingredients including the apples. Then pour the liquid ingredients into the dry ingredients. Mix until everything is moistened. Scoop into muffin tins and bake 15 to 25 minutes until golden brown. Serve cool to horses. Serve warm to people!

Apple Roses

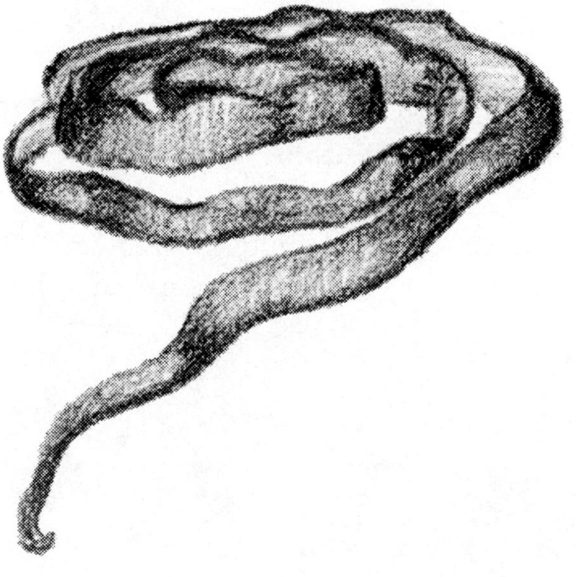

Using a potato peeler, carefully peel skin slowly off an apple in one continuous spiral string.

Arrange peel in a circle to make a rose. For added color, place a red seedless grape in the center.

This garnish is very fragile, make directly over bran mash for a special treat.

Recipes reprinted with permission from *The Original Book of Horse Treats* by June V. Evers.
See page 64 to order the book.

How Does a Horse Sleep?

Humans tend to get their sleep in 6-8 hour stretches, usually at night. Even though horses live and work with humans, they still follow the same sleep pattern that helped them survive in the wild. Understanding a horse's sleep habits will help you enjoy your own horse.

First, horses don't need as much sleep as humans. A horse needs only about 4 hours of sleep in a 24-hour period. Instead of taking a long 4-hour nap, the typical horse takes short 30-minute "power naps" throughout the day. In the wild, horses lived in wide-open spaces and always had to be on the lookout for hungry predators. Short naps helped wild horses keep alert for danger so they didn't end up being some other animal's dinner.

Horses do some of their sleeping during the day. Most horses lie down for a day-time nap, especially outdoors when the weather is sunny. Lying down was a big danger for wild horses if a predator were close by. It would take many seconds for the horse to stand up and prepare to run away. Horses adapted to this problem with changes in their skeleton, allowing them to sleep standing up.

The horse's ability to sleep standing up is a valuable safety feature leftover from living in the wild. Horses have a special locking joint in their elbows and stifles. When a horse sleeps standing up, these joints lock. This supports the horse on its forehand (front quarters). A horse can even rest one hind leg while sleeping and not fall over. When a horse is alerted to danger, its head comes up. This action throws the horse's weight to its hindquarters and the horse is ready to gallop to safety.

Scientists report that horses (and humans) experience two kinds of sleep. SWS stands for short wave sleep. This kind of sleep is shallow, more like dozing. Horses often do this standing up and can be easily awakened from SWS. REM stands for rapid eye movement sleep. During this kind of sleep, the eyes move rapidly from side to side behind the eyelids. During REM sleep the brain waves are longer and the body is completely relaxed. Scientists suggest that horses lay down to experience REM sleep. Lying down in REM sleep, a horse is easy to approach but is not easily awakened.

Because of their sleep habits, horse owners must make sure they have provided their horse the opportunity to rest comfortably. A stalled horse should be kept in a stall large enough to allow it to lie flat out and experience REM sleep. A horse that lies down in a stall that is too small may become 'cast.' This happens when the horse rolls over and becomes trapped on its back next to the wall of the stall. You must also pay special attention a horse's bedding. The stall bedding needs to be dry, soft and clean to encourage the horse to lie down.

Horses spending time outside also need a smooth dry spot to lie down. Extremely wet ground may keep a horse from lying down and it may

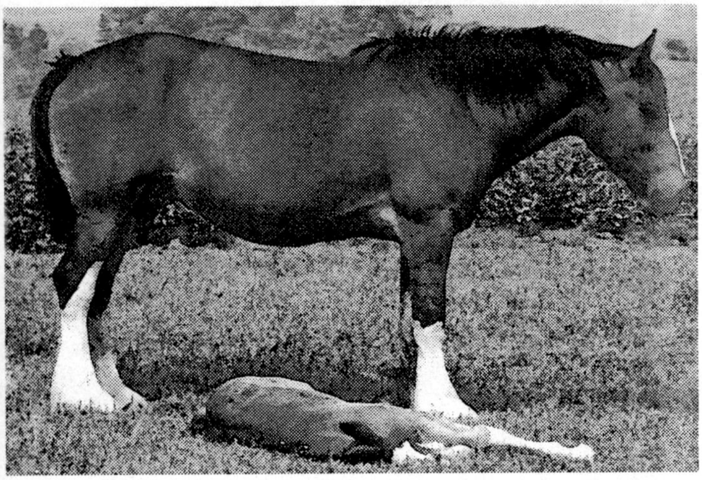

This mare is dozing, probably having SWS sleep. The foal is stretched flat out in REM sleep.

Across

5 These kinds of animals hunt other creatures for food. (9)
7 Horses lived in these kind of spaces in the wild. (4,4)
9 A term for when a horse gets trapped on its back in a stall. (4)
11 Horses often sleep while doing this. (8,2)
12 What SWS stands for. (8,2)
13 The length of a typical horse nap. (6,7)

Down

1 You should do this at a horse show to give your horse a chance to rest. (8)
2 These special kinds of joints are found in a horse's elbow and stifle. (7)
3 Horses need about this many hours of sleep in a 24 hour time span. (4)
4 Another term for a horse's front quarters. (8)
6 Short naps helped wild horses keep _________ for danger. (5)
8 A horse's usual reaction to danger. (3,4)
10 A horse in REM sleep is not easily _________. (8)

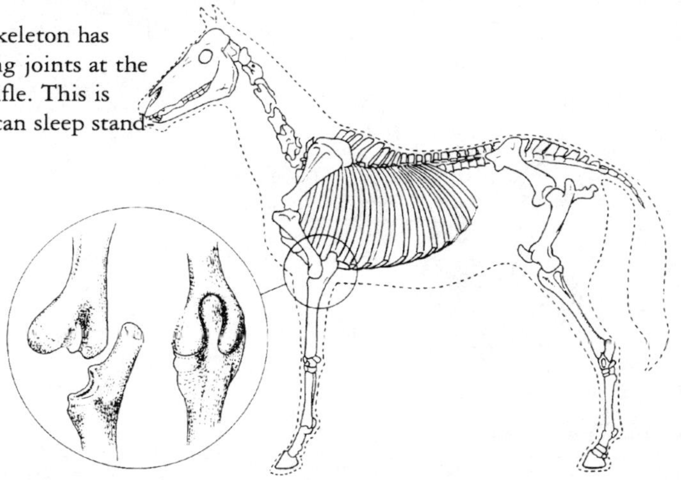

The horse's skeleton has special locking joints at the elbow and stifle. This is why a horse can sleep standing up.

lose sleep. During winter or other wet times of the year, horse owners should provide a run-in
or other shelter where horses can choose to nap.

At horse shows and other competitive events, it is very important to give your horse an opportunity to take a nap. Dismount if you are not practicing or competing (your horse is not a lawnchair!). Loosen the girth or untack your horse so that it relaxes and knows that it can take a break.

A happy, healthy, well-rested horse is the best equine companion. Make sure your horse gets the sleep he needs.

Buiding Fences and Jumps

If you have model horses, you have probably been trying to figure out how to buy or make fences and jumps for them. It's easy! Just collect popsicle sticks, markers or paint, and glue.

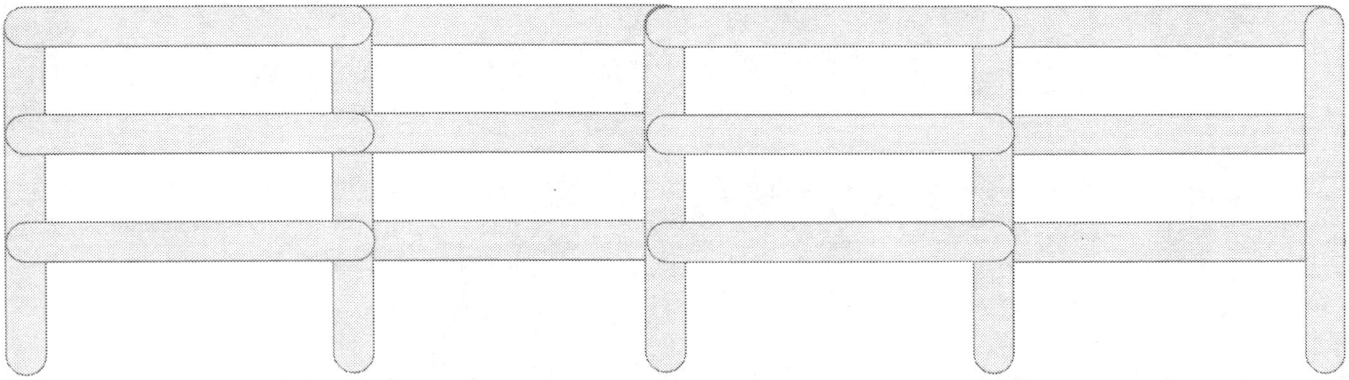

When stacked, if you look at the edges, this is what you'll see.

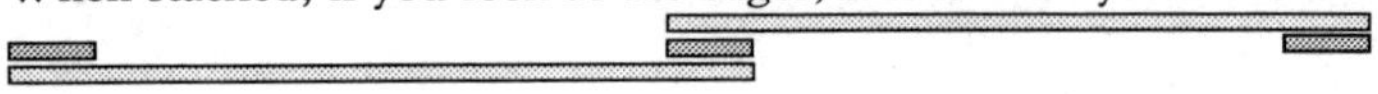

Arrange popsicle sticks with two or three rows of "boards" and three or four "posts".

Jumps have two posts and as many boards as you like. The height of the jump comes from where the board is attached.

Put a drop of glue where each stick lays on another. Let it dry for a few hours. Now they're ready for some color!

To stand up a fence or jump, roll a ball of clay or play dough for each post, and push onto the base of each post. Stand the fence up on wax paper and use your thumbs and first fingers to press the ball into a pyramid. Let it dry overnight. When dry, peel off the wax paper and lay it on it's side to finish drying inside.

Play Dough

$1\frac{1}{2}$ cups flour
$\frac{3}{4}$ cups salt
3 teaspoons cream of tartar (or arrowroot)
$1\frac{1}{2}$ cups cool water
$1\frac{1}{2}$ tablespoons oil
food coloring

Mix dry ingredients together in a cooking pot. Blend all liquids together in a bowl. Combine the liquids with the dry ingredients and mix throughly. Cook over medium heat, stirring constantly. Remove from heat when dough pulls away from the sides of the pot and can be pinched without sticking (about 5 minutes). Turn onto board or counter and knead until smooth and play dough consistency. Store in airtight container.

Reading List

Your local library will have many of these wonderful books. As you read them, check the box to the right. If you have some in your own collection, check those boxes too.

Author	Title (year first published)	I Have it	I Read it
Alder, C.S.	More Than A Horse (1997)		
	That Horse Whiskey (1994)		
Aldridge, James	The Broken Saddle (1982)		
	A Sporting Proposition (1973)		
Ankskarv ard, Karin	Rider by Night (1960)		
Anderson, C. W.	Afraid to Ride (1957)		
	Billy and Blaze (1936)		
	Blaze and the Forest Fire (1938)		
	Blaze and the Gray Spotted Pony (1968)		
	Blaze and the Gypsies (1937)		
	Blaze and the Indian Cave (1964)		
	Blaze and the Lost Quarry (1966)		
	Blaze and the Mountain Lion (1959)		
	Blaze and Thunderbolt (1955)		
	Blaze Finds the Trail (1950)		
	Blaze Shows the Way (1969)		
	The Blind Connemara (1971)		
	The Crooked Colt (1954)		
	A Filly for Joan (1960)		
Bagnold, Enid	National Velvet (1949)		
Bailey, Jean	Cherokee Bill, Oklahoma Pacer (1970)		
Baker, Karen	Senecca (1997)		
Balch, Glenn	Indian Paint, the Story of an Indian Pony (1942)		
	Stallion's Foe (1963)		
	Tiger Roan (1938)		
Beatty, Hetty Burlingame	Blitz (1961)		
Benedict, Dorthy Pott	Fabulous (1961)		
Bently, Karen	Arabian Challenge (1997)		
	Ashleigh's Farewell (1996)		
	Champion's Spirit (1997)		
	Cindy's Heartbreak (1997)		
	Glory in Danger (1996)		
	Glory's Rival (1997)		
	Glory's Triumph (1996)		
	Samantha's Journey (1997)		
	Wonder's Champion (1997)		
Bialk, Elisa	The Colt of Cripple Creek (1953)		
	The Horse Called Pete (1948)		
	Tizz at the Stampede (1968)		
	Tizz Plays Santa Claus (1957)		
	Wild Horse Island (1951)		
Blanc, Esther Silverst	Berchink (1989)		
Bodker, Cecil	Silas and the Ben-Godik (1978)		
	Silas and the Black Mare (1978)		
Bradbury, Bianca,	My Pretty Girl (1974)		
Brett, Jan	Fritz and the Beautiful Horses (1981)		
Brown, Beth	All Horses Go to Heaven; an Anthology of Short Stories (1963)		
	The Wonderful World of Horses (1967)		
Brown, Eleanor Frances	The Colt From Horse Heaven Hills (1956)		
	A Horse for Peter (1950)		
Brown, Fern G.	Hard Luck Horse (1975)		
Bryant, Bonnie	Autumn Trail (1993)		
	Beach Ride (1993)		
	Before They Rode Horses (1997)		
	Bridle Path (1993)		
	Broken Horse (1996)		
	Chocolate Horse (1994)		
	Cutting Horse (1996)		
	Dream Horse (1996)		
	Endurance Ride (1997)		
	English Horse (1998)		

Author	Title (year first published)	I Have it	I Read it
Bryant, Bonnie	English Rider (1998)		
	Flying Horse (1995)		
	Fox Hunt (1992)		
	Ghost Rider (1992)		
	Gift Horse (1995)		
	Gold Medal Horse (1996)		
	Gold Medal Rider (1996)		
	Hay Fever (1994)		
	Hayride (1993)		
	High Horse (1994)		
	Hobbyhorse (1996)		
	Holiday Horse (1997)		
	Horse Blues (1997)		
	Horse Capades (1997)		
	Horse Care (1998)		
	Horse Crazy (1988)		
	Horse Fever (1999)		
	Horse Games (1991)		
	Horse Quest (1998)		
	Horse Magic (1995)		
	Horse Race (1997)		
	Horse Sense (1989)		
	Horse Shy (1988)		
	Horse-Sitters (1996)		
	Horse Tale (1994)		
	Horse Talk (1997)		
	Horse Thief (1998)		
	Horse Trade (1994)		
	Horse Trouble (1992)		
	Horse Whispers (1998)		
	Horseflies (1998)		
	Horsesnapped (1991)		
	Horseshoe (1995)		
	The Long Ride (1998)		
	Mystery Ride (1995)		
	Nightmare (1997)		
	Pack Trip (1991)		
	Painted Horse (1998)		
	Photo Finish (1995)		
	Pleasure Horse (1996)		
	Purebred (1994)		
	Quarter Horse (1998)		
	Racehorse (1992)		
	Ranch Hands (1993)		
	Riding Class (1996)		
	Riding Lesson (1994)		
	Rocking Horse (1998)		
	Saddle Sore (1997)		
	Saddlebags (1995)		
	Schooling Horse (1998)		
	Secret Horse (1999)		
	The Secret of the Stallion (1995)		
	Silver Stirrups (1997)		
	Snow Ride (1992)		
	Stable Farewell (1995)		
	Stable Groom (1995)		
	Stable Hearts (1997)		
	Stable Manners (1993)		
	Stable Witch (1995)		
	Stage Coach (1994)		
	Stevie: the Inside Story (1999)		
	Summer Horse (1997)		
	A Summer Without Horses (1994)		

Author	Title (year first published)	I Have it	I Read it
Bryant, Bonnie	Tight Rein (1996)	☐	☐
	Wagon Trail (1998)	☐	☐
	Western Star (1995)	☐	☐
	Wild Horses (1996)	☐	☐
	Yankee Swap (1995)	☐	☐
Bulla, Clyde Robert	Star of the Wild Horse Canyon (1953)	☐	☐
Byars, Betsy Cromer	The Winged Colt of Casa Mia (1975)	☐	☐
Calvert, Patricia	The Snowbird (1980)	☐	☐
Campell, Barbara	A Girl Called Bob & a Horse	☐	☐
	Called Yoki (1982)	☐	☐
Campell, Joanna	Ashleigh's Christmas Miracle (1994)	☐	☐
	Ashleigh's Diary (1995)	☐	☐
	Ashleigh's Dream (1993)	☐	☐
	Ashleigh's Hope (1996)	☐	☐
	Cindy's Runaway Colt (1995)	☐	☐
	A Horse Called Wonder (1991)	☐	☐
	Pride's Challenge (1994)	☐	☐
	Pride's Last Race (1994)	☐	☐
	Samatha's Pride (1993)	☐	☐
	Shining's Orphan (1995)	☐	☐
	Sierra's Steeplechase (1993)	☐	☐
	The Wild Mustang (1989)	☐	☐
	Wonder's First Race (1993)	☐	☐
	Wonder' Promise (1991)	☐	☐
	Wonder's Sister (1994)	☐	☐
	Wonder's Victory (1991)	☐	☐
	Wonder's Yearling (1993)	☐	☐
Carroll, Ruth	Tough Enough's Pony (1958)	☐	☐
Cavanna, Betty	Banner Year (1987)	☐	☐
	Wanted: a Girl for the Horses (1984)	☐	☐
Cherryh, C.J.	Rider at the Gate (1995)	☐	☐
Choldenko, Gennifer	Moonstruck: the True Story of the Cow Who... (1996)	☐	☐
Christiansen, Candace	The Ice Horse (1993)	☐	☐
Cohen, Peter Zachary	Bee (1975)	☐	☐
	Calm Horses (1982)	☐	☐
Corbin, William	Golden Mare (1955)	☐	☐
Damrell, Liz	With the Wind (1991)	☐	☐
Dennis, Wesley	Flip (1941)	☐	☐
	Flip and the Cows; Story and Pictures (1942)	☐	☐
	Flip and the Morning (1951)	☐	☐
Dickerson, Karie	The Forgotten Filly (1993)	☐	☐
Doherty, Berlie	Snowy (1993)	☐	☐
Dolan, Shelia	The Wishing Bottle (1979)	☐	☐
Dolch, Edward W.	Horse Stories in Basic Vocabulary (1958)	☐	☐
Doty, Jean Slaughter	The Crumb (1976)	☐	☐
	Dark Horse (1951)	☐	☐
	If Wishes Were Horses (1993)	☐	☐
	The Monday Horses (1993)	☐	☐
	Summer Pony (1979)	☐	☐
	The Valley of the Ponies (1958)	☐	☐
	Winter Pony (1976)	☐	☐
	Yesterday's Horses (1983)	☐	☐
Downey, Fairfax Davis	My Kingdom for a Horse (1984)	☐	☐
Dunn, Marylois	The Absolutely Perfect Horse (1978)	☐	☐
Eames, Genevieve Torre	Flying Roundup (1973)	☐	☐
Esstman, Barbara	Night Ride Home (1982)	☐	☐
Estes, Allison	Gold Medal Mystery (1975)	☐	☐
Ets, Marie Hall	Mister Penny's Race Horse (1985)	☐	☐
Evans, Pauline Rush	Best Book of Horse Stories (1964)	☐	☐
Faralla, Dana	Black Renegade (1954)	☐	☐
	The Magnificent Barb (1947)	☐	☐
Farley, Steven	The Black Stallion's Shadow (1996)	☐	☐
Farley, Walter	Big Black Horse (1953)	☐	☐
	The Black Stallion (1941)	☐	☐
	The Black Stallion and Flame (1986)	☐	☐
	The Black Stallion and Satan (1949)	☐	☐
	The Black Stallion and the Girl (1971)	☐	☐
	The Black Stallion Challenged! (1964)	☐	☐

Author	Title (year first published)	I Have it	I Read it
Farley, Walter	The Black Stallion Legend (1983)	☐	☐
	The Black Stallion Mystery (1957)	☐	☐
	The Black Stallion Returns (1945)	☐	☐
	The Black Stallion Revolts (1953)	☐	☐
	The Black Stallion's Blood Bay Colt (1978)	☐	☐
	The Black Stallion's Courage (1956)	☐	☐
	The Black Stallion's Filly (1952)	☐	☐
	The Black Stallion's Ghost (1969)	☐	☐
	The Black Stallion's Sulky Colt (1950)	☐	☐
	The Blood Bay Colt (1950)	☐	☐
	The Horse-Tamer (1958)	☐	☐
	The Island Stallion (1948)	☐	☐
	The Island Stallion Races (1955)	☐	☐
	The Island Stallion's Fury (1951)	☐	☐
	Little Black, a Pony (1961)	☐	☐
	Little Black Goes to the Circus (1963)	☐	☐
	Man O' War (1962)	☐	☐
	Son of the Black Stallion (1947)	☐	☐
	The Young Black Stallion (1989)	☐	☐
Fenner, Carol	Lagalag, the Wanderer (1968)	☐	☐
	A Summer of Horses (1989)	☐	☐
Fenner, Phyllis R.	Gentle Like a Cyclone: Stories of Horses (1974)	☐	☐
	Horses, Horses, Horses: Palominos and Pint (1949)	☐	☐
Forbus, Ina B.	Tawny's Trick (1965)	☐	☐
Foster, John T.	The Gallant Gay Trotter (1974)	☐	☐
Friedrich, Elizabeth	Leah's Pony (1996)	☐	☐
Friskey, Margaret	Indian Two Feet and His Horse (1959)	☐	☐
Furman, A.L.	More Horse Stories (1966)	☐	☐
Gard, Robert Edward	A Horse Named Joe (1956)	☐	☐
Garlnd, Sherry	Best Horse on the Force (1991)	☐	☐
Gates, Dorris	Little Vic (1951)	☐	☐
	A Morgan for Melinda: a Novel (1980)	☐	☐
Gauch, Patricia Lee	The Year the Summer Died (1985)	☐	☐
Gipson, Fred	Little Arliss (1978)	☐	☐
Goble, Paul	The Gift of the Sacred Dog (1980)	☐	☐
Golden, Lilly	The Literary Horse: Great Modern Stories (1995)	☐	☐
Gray, Patsey	The Flag is Up (1970)	☐	☐
	Loco, the Bronc (1961)	☐	☐
Green, Timothy	Twilight Boy (1998)	☐	☐
Griffith, Helen V.	The Last Summer: Spain 1936 (1979)	☐	☐
Gruenberg, Linda	Hummer (1990)	☐	☐
Haas, Jessie	Be Well, Beware (1996)	☐	☐
	Beware and Stogie (1998)	☐	☐
	Beware the Mare (1993)	☐	☐
	A Horse Like Barney (1993)	☐	☐
	Keeping Barney (1981)	☐	☐
	No Foal Yet (1995)	☐	☐
	Sugaring (1996)	☐	☐
	Uncle Danny's Way (1994)	☐	☐
Hader, Berta	Little Appaloosa (1949)	☐	☐
Hall, Lynn	Danza! (1981)	☐	☐
	Dragon Defiant (1983)	☐	☐
	Flying Changes (1991)	☐	☐
	The Horse Trader (1981)	☐	☐
	New Day for Dragon (1975)	☐	☐
	Ride a Dark Horse (1987)	☐	☐
	Ride a Wild Dream (1969)	☐	☐
Hart, Alison	Andie Out of Control (1994)	☐	☐
	Andie Shows Off (1994)	☐	☐
	Andie's Risky Business (1995)	☐	☐
Hays, Wilma Pitchford	The Little Horse That Raced a Train (1959)	☐	☐
Heilbroner, Joan	Robert the Rose Horse (1962)	☐	☐
Hendry, Frances	Quest for a Kelpie (1988)	☐	☐
Henry, Marguerite	Black Gold (1957)	☐	☐
	Born to Trot (1950)	☐	☐
	Gaudnezia: Pride of the Palio (1960)	☐	☐
	Justin Morgan Had a Horse (1945)	☐	☐
	King of the Wind (1948)Henry, Marguerite	☐	☐

Author	Title (year first published)	I Have it	I Read it
	The Little Fellow (1945)		
	Misty of Chincoteague (1947)		
	Misty's Twilight (1992)		
gdon, Hal	The Horse That Played Center Field (1968)		
nton, S. E.	Taming the Star Runner (1988)		
berman, Mary Ann	Mr. and Mrs. Muddle (1988)		
ff, Syd	Barney's Horse: Story and Pictures (1987)		
	Chester (1961)		
	Thunderhoof (1971)		
gner, Nils	The Nosy Colt (1973)		
ke, Helen	The Horse That Takes the Milk Around (1946)		
lland, Isabelle	A Horse Named Peaceable (1982)		
nnson, Patricia H.	The Sweet Running Filly (1971)		
hnson, Virginia Weis	The Cedars of Charlo (1969)		
lnay, Francis	Chucaro, Wild Pony of the Pampa (1958)		
nno, Wendy	Sampson the Horse (1984)		
owles, Anne	Under the Shadow (1983)		
Farge, Phyllis	Joanna Runs Away (1973)		
rom, Henry V.	Mountain Pony (1946)		
wson, Robert	Mr. Revere and I (1953)		
Guin, Ursula K.	A Ride on the Red Mare's Back (1992)		
itch, Patricia	The Fields of Praise (1978)		
	Mystery Horse (1995)		
	Show Jumper Wanted (1995)		
ngstrand, Rolf	The Long Pony Race (1966)		
Vert, Suzanne	Great Horse Stories (1984)		
vin, Betty	Gift Horse (1996)		
vy, Elizabeth	Something Queer in the Wild West (1997)		
cker, Thomas	The Mare on the Hill (1985)		
ndon, Sara	Firehorse Max (1997)		
ons, Dorthy	Dark Sunshine (1951)		
ason, Miriam Evangeli	Broomtail, Brother of Lightning (1952)		
cCaffrey, Anne	Black Horse for the King (1996)		
eader, Stephe W.	Red horse Hill (1930)		
eigs, Cornelia	The Dutch Colt (1952)		
erill, Jean	The Superlative Horse (1961)		
les, Miska	Pony in the Schoolhouse (1964)		
ller, Albert G.	Fury: Stallion of Broken Wheel Ranch (1959)		
tchell, Elynne	The Man From Snowy River (1982)		
eri, Louise	A Horse for X.Y.Z. (1977)		
ore, Lilian	Old Rosie: the Horse Nobody Understood (1960)		
ore, Mavis Garey	Pony for a Prize (1951)		
rey, Walt	Runaway Stallion (1973)		
	Year of the Black Pony (1976)		
rgenroth, Barbara	Impossible Charlie (1979)		
	Last Junior Year (1978)		
	Ride a Proud Horse (1978)		
rpugo, Michael	War Horse (1983)		
rrison, Dorothy Nafu	Whisper Goodbye (1985)		
bb, Magdalen	The Enchanted Horse (1993)		
Hara, Mary	My Friend Flicka (1941)		
	Thunderhead (1943)		
dham, Mary	The White Pony (1981)		
ver, Marjorie Mary	Riding Days (1948)		
o, Margaret Glover	Cocoa (1953)		
ce, Mildred Mastin	Old Bones, the Wonder Horse (1955)		
azzo, Tony	Charley the Horse (1950)		
ck, Robert Newton	The Horse Hunters (1988)		
	Spanish Hoof (1985)		
et, Bill	Cowardly Clyde (1979)		
terson, Jeanne White	Sometimes I Dream Horses (1987)		
yton, K.M.	The Team (1976)		
ilbrick, W.R.	The Fire Pony (1996)		
tt, Chris	Willow King (1998)		
acco, Patricia	Mrs. Mack (1998)		
te, Barbara Ann	Harry's Pony (1997)		
merva, Elise	Basil & Maggie (1983)		
dmond, Dianne	The Most beautiful Horse in the World (1994)		

Author	Title (year first published)	I Have it	I Read it
Reid, Barbara	Miguel and His Racehorse (1973)		
Reyonolds, Marjorie	Keep a Silver Dollar (1966)		
Rivers-Coffey, Rachel	A Horse Like Ragman (1977)		
Roberts, Lillian M.	Riding for a Fall (1996)		
Rock, Gail	The Thanksgiving Treasure (1974)		
Rockwood, Joyce	Groundhog's Horse (1978)		
Rosenberg, Liz	The Carousel (1995)		
Rosenthal, Chuck	Elena of the Stars (1995)		
Rottman, S. L.	Hero (1997)		
Rounds, Glen	The Blind Colt (1960)		
	Blind Outlaw (1980)		
	Hunted Horses (1951)		
	Once We Had a Horse (1996)		
	Stolen Pony (1969)		
	Whitey and the Wild Horse (1958)		
	Wild Appaloosa (1983)		
Ruepp, Krista	Midnight Rider (1995)		
Sanderson, William E.	Nez Perce Buffalo Horse (1972)		
Savage, Deborah	Under a Different Sky (1997)		
Savitt, Sam	Vicki and the Brown Mare (1976)		
	Wild Horse Running (1973)		
Saxon, Nancy	Pinky in the Saddle (1984)		
Scott, Sally	Chica (1954)		
Seligman, Dorthy Hall	The Trouble With Horses (1971)		
Sewall, Marica	Ridin' That Strawberry Roan (1985)		
Sewell, Ann	Black Beauty (1941)		
	Black Beauty: His Grooms and Companions (1990)		
	Black Beauty:the Autobiography of a Horse (1945)		
Shapiro, Irwin	Gretchen and the White Steed (1972)		
Shub, Elizabeth	The White Stallion (1982)		
Slade, Michael	The Horses of Central Park (1992)		
Smith, Eunice Young	Shoon, Wild Pony of the Moors (1965)		
Smith, Vian Crocker	Green Heart (1964)		
	Martin Rides the Moor (1965)		
	The Minstrel Boy (1970)		
Snyder, Zilpha Keatley	Gib Rides Home (1998)		
Spinka, Penina Keen	White Hare's Horses (1991)		
Springer, Nancy	The Boy on a Black Horse (1994)		
	Colt (1991)		
Steinbeck, John	The Red Pony (1945)		
Stevenson, Carol Dornf	Stubborn Binnder (1961)		
Stone, Eugenia	Sagebrush Filly (1950)		
Strachan, Margaret Pit	Mystery At Blue Barn Stables (1970)		
Thiele, Colin	Jodie's Journey (1990)		
Thomas, David	Horse Stories (1964)		
Thomas, Joyce Carol	The Golden Pasture (1986)		
	Three Great Horse Stories (1957)		
Tousey, Sanford	Horseman Hal (1950)		
Towne, Mary	Boxed In (1982)		
Tremble, Freda B.	Modoc (1972)		
Tripp, Valerie	Meet Felicity: An American Girl (1991)		
Turnbull, Ann	The Sandhorse (1989)		
Vail, Virginia	If Wishes Were Horses (1994)		
Van der Veer, Judy	Hold the Rein Free (1966)		
Viereck, Philip	Sue's Secondhand Horse (1973)		
Waddell, Martin	Harriet and the Haunted School (1984)		
Walker, Diana	Mother Wants a Horse (1978)		
	The Year of the Horse (1975)		
Wallace, Bill	Beauty (1988)		
Welch, Sheila Keely	A Horse For All Seasons: Collected Stories (1994)		
Williams, J.R.	The Horse-Talker (1960)		
Williama, Ursula Moray	No Ponies For Miss Pobjoy (1975)		
Wojciechowska, Maia	A Kingdom in the Horse (1965)		
Wormser, Richard E.	The Black Mustanger (1971)		
Young, Miriam	If I Rode a Horse (1973)		

Puzzle Answers

p.3

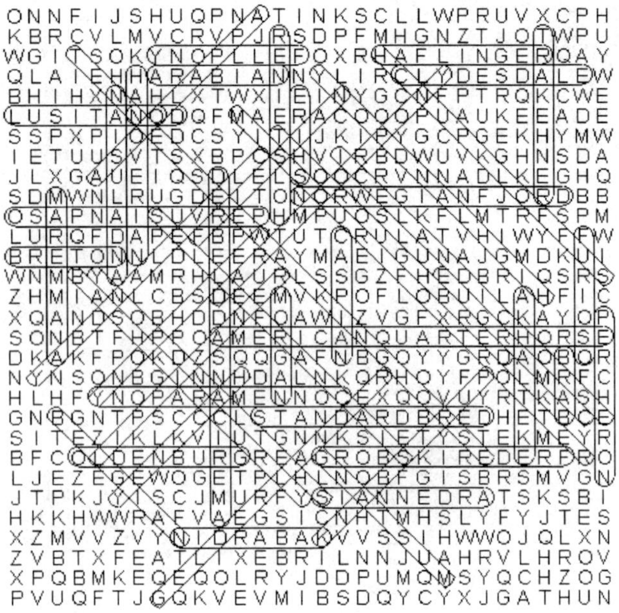

p.5

p.7

p.9

p.11

p.13

p.15

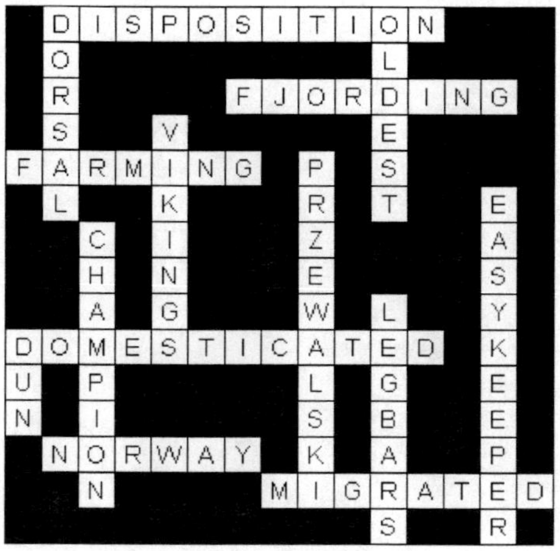

p.17

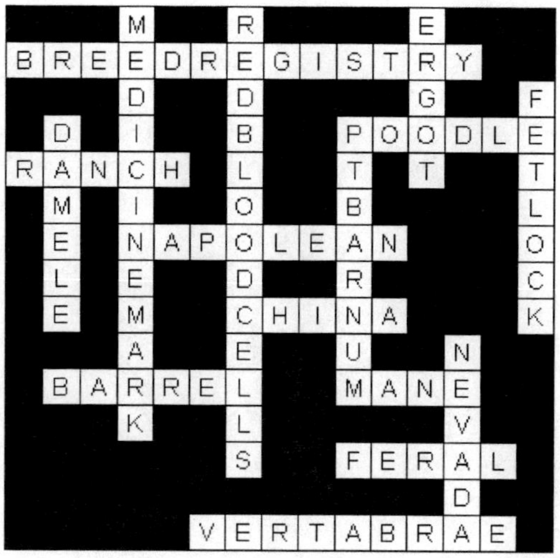

p.20

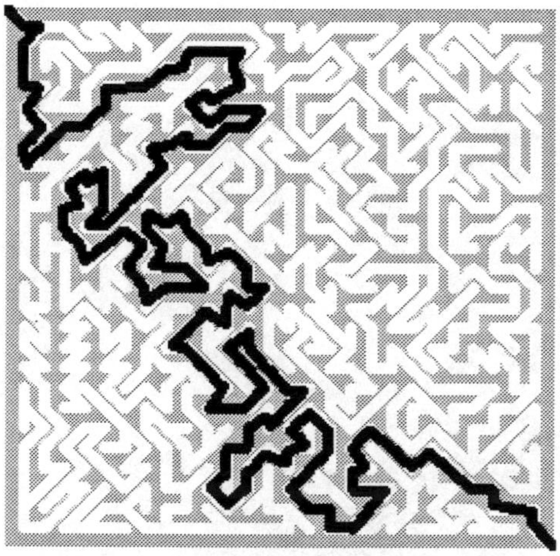

p.22-23

A - T
B - T
C - O
D - T
E - T
F - O
G - T

p.25

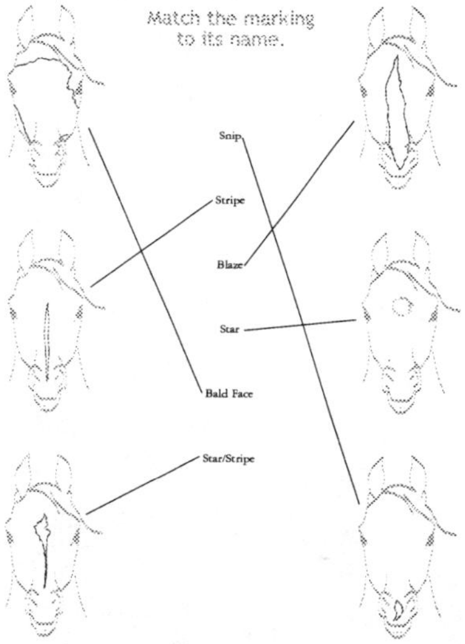

p.27

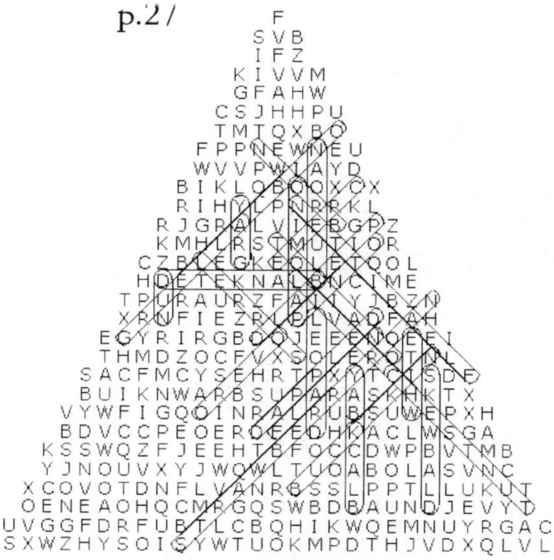

p.33

Puzzle Answers

p.35

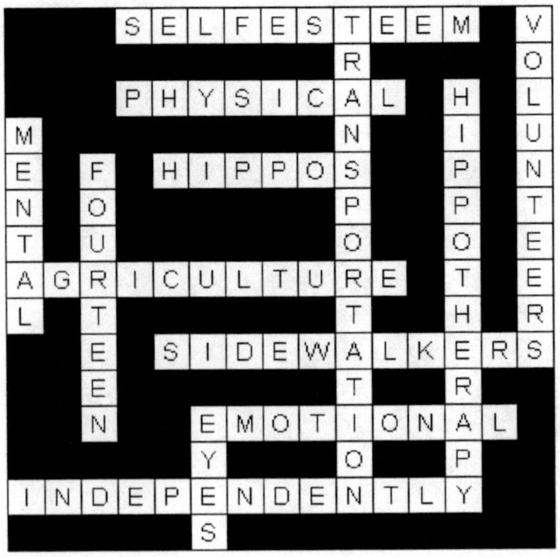

p.37

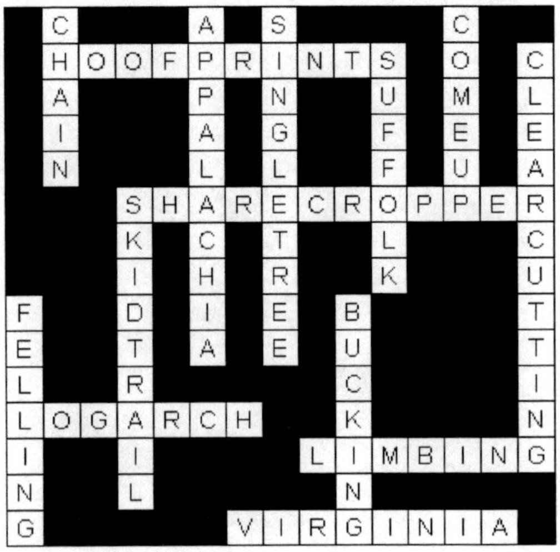

p.38

To a retail store.

p.41

p.39

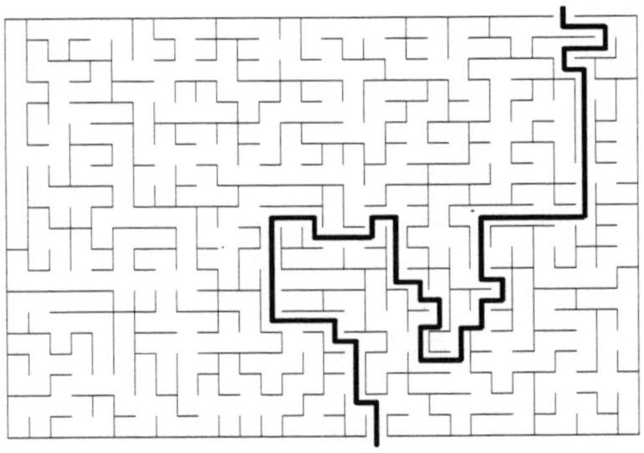

p.43

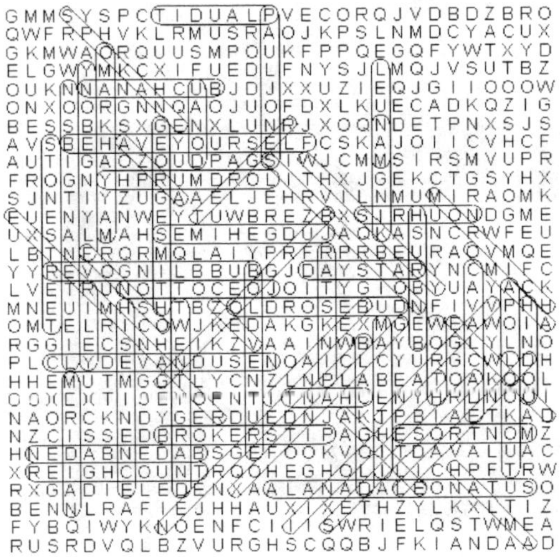

p.44

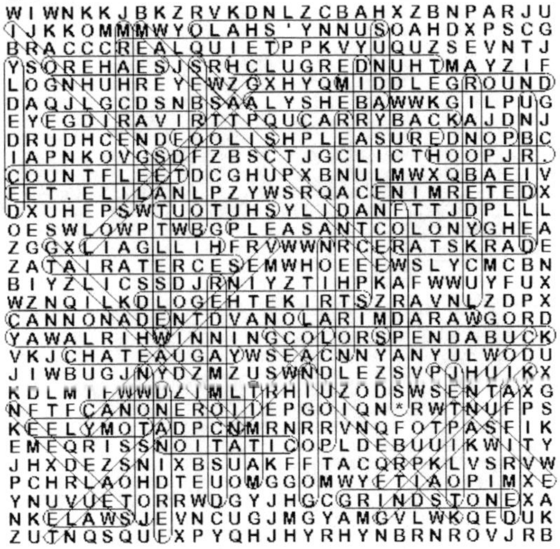

p.45

p.47

p.48

His horse's name was Friday.

p.53

Illustration Credits

Page	Provided by
2	International Museum of the Horse, Randy Womack

All other illustrations by Kimberly Spatrisano-Graham

Photo Credits

Page	Provided by
4	Corel Stock Photography
6	Diamonds Ranch
7	J. Eastcott & Y. Momatiuk
8-9	Shawn Hamilton, CLiX Photography
10-11	International Museum of the Horse, Corel Stock Photography
12-13	Oklahoma State University, Heroden Stud, Icelandic Horse Farm, National Chincoteague Pony Assn., Beaverwood Farms
14	Reflection of Killington, Inc.
16-17	Kim Marie Wood
20-21	Susan Dudasik, Corel Stock Photography
22-23	APHA, Barlink Ranch, Diamonds Ranch, KDL Ranch, Painted Pony Horse Ranch
24	Doug Wood
26	Kimberly Graham
28-29	Kimberly Graham & Kim Wood
30-31	Corel Stock Photography
34-35	Kim Marie Wood
36-37	CLiX Photography
40-41	Kimberly Graham, Kim Marie Wood
42-45	Belmont
48	R. Hess
49	Kim Marie Wood

Coming Soon

More books by Kim Marie Wood

Forelocks, Fetlocks and Horse Tales is a collection of ten short fiction stories, each with an equine angle. Written for middle grade readers, it will be a perfect gift for the young horse lover in your life.

Something unique and magical happens between girls and their horses. **Heart, Hoof & Soul** is a collection of true stories about these special relationships.

Posters Available

"Childhood Dreams"

Original - Pastels

Poster
24½" x 24"
Bright Colors
$9.95

"Ghostly White"
Original - Pen & Ink

Poster
18" x 24"
Black & White
$4.95

The Power of Horses Order Form

Syncopated PRESS

Syncopated Press
P.O. Box 411
Plainwell, MI 49080
fax: 616-685-6765

Name: ______________________ Phone: (   )

Address: ______________________ Fax #: (   )

City: ______________________ State/Prov.:

Country: ______________________ Postal Code/Zip:

Quantity		Amount	Total
___	The Power of Horses	$ 14.95	______
___	"Childhood Dreams" Poster	9.95	______
___	"Ghostly White" Poster	4.95	______
	Michigan Residents add Sales Tax	6%	______
	Shipping (per item)	3.50	______
	All sales in U.S. Dollars	Total Due	

Payment by: VISA MC Check Money Order

Card # ______________________ Expiration Date:

Card Holder Signature ______________________

Card Holder Name (please print) ______________________
(Required for credit card authorizations to ship)

The Original Book of Horse Treats Order Form

The Original Book of Horse Treats is a compilation of serious and fun recipes that you can make at home for your horse. Create horse-tastey treats such as Stuffed Molasses Apples, Bran Mashes and Sundae Supreme. Filled with illustrations and photographs, this beautifully designed book has over 70 recipes. There is even a terrific section on home-made liniments, fly sprays and hoof oils. Bound with sturdy spiral wire makes this book easy to use in your kitchen. Don't miss out on this must-have for horse lovers!

Horse Hollow Press
27 Main St.
Chester NY. 10918
Phone: 1-800-4-1-HORSE (46773)
FAX: 914-469-2389

Name: ______________________ Daytime Phone:(   )

Address: ______________________ Fax #:(   )

City: ______________________ State/Prov.:

Country: ______________________ Postal Code/Zip:

Quantity		Amount	Total
___	The Original Book of Horse Treats	$ 19.95	______
	New York Residents add Sales Tax	7.25%	______
	Shipping (per item)	4.50	______
	All sales in U.S. Dollars	Total Due	

Standard UPS   2-day air   Next day air   First Class Mail

Payment by: VISA   MC   Check   Money Order

Card #   Expiration Date:

Card Holder Signature

Card Holder Name (please print)

(Required for credit card authorizations to ship)